Glenn Miller's *The Prophetic Fall of the Islamic Regime* is brilliant! Glenn is a master at weighing the facts on God's scales. The results are frightening and sobering. Babylon, historically and prophetically, has produced dictators who have ruled over kings, leaders, nations, and religions. The shores of the free are never completely at rest because of the constant desire of this spirit to rob the people who know their God, from joy, hope, and spiritual expression. Like other false deities mentioned in the Bible, however, these gods are powerless to deliver mankind from the grip of sin. They seek only to subvert God's righteous purposes.

Even if there was an ounce of truth in the Quran, the god of Islam would fall down and bow, but unfortunately, there is no truth because the knowledge of real truth sets one free.

In prophetic fashion, Glenn has put pen to paper, and we believe that as a result souls will begin to hunger for the true God even in the presence of oppressive dictators. Even though they claim that Allah makes it easy for the righteous when they die, most of those who have been stung by the scorpion of this lie long for peace and freedom while on this earth and are compelled to believe that they have to kill or destroy those "who believe not" (Surah 6:126) in order to hold a special place in heaven.

Billions of souls are ready for Christ, and ? lays out the simple "A-B-C's" of salvation. again reminded of the simplicity of rec through Christ. Why would anyone a beautiful gift?

We live in time, and time ca at limits our understanding of the wor. Glenn Miller states in *The Prophetic Fall of the i. gime*, "Only God can accurately interpret history. Th. is where the prophetic voice in the earth becomes invaluable."

This book is quite amazing and filled with revelation. God expects His people to respond to Him out of the time frame and season in which we live on the earth. We respond through prophetic intercession, declaration, and apostolic proclamation. To respond properly, we must have revelation so that when we decree a thing it will come to pass.

We are moving into a season of confrontation. We will confront the enemies of God's covenant plan by releasing the revelation of His covenant against every anti-Christ force in the earth.

Glenn also shares that "when God invades a culture He will break off the darkness so He can bring the light of the saving grace of His Son." We are moving toward a great clash of the kingdoms. This book will be a tremendous help to many so that we can *see* God moving and revealed in current events. I highly recommend this book to those who will be leaders in God's army. I also fully recommend this work to every God-called intercessor and prophetic watchman who will stand in the gap on behalf of the harvest of the nations in the days ahead.

—CHUCK D. PIERCE
PRESIDENT, GLORY OF ZION
INTERNATIONAL MINISTRIES, INC.
VICE PRESIDENT, GLOBAL HARVEST MINISTRIES

This book will *speed* up your understanding of what is about to happen in our world. This book will help you know what God is about to do in this life. You hold in your hand a revealing book about prophecy that will move you like no other book. Read and believe because Glenn Miller has heard from God.

—PASTOR STEVE MUNSEY
FAMILY CHRISTIAN CENTER
MUNSTER, IN

The Prophetic Fall of the Islamic Regime is a timely book. With so much focus on Muslims in the news media, many Christians are confused as to what to think about Islam. Glenn Miller helps us enormously to clarify the issues and to see Islam for what it is. I was especially pleased that he is so forthright in explaining that "Allah" is not God, but rather an emissary of darkness. This book will strengthen our faith.

—C. PETER WAGNER, CHANCELLOR
WAGNER LEADERSHIP INSTITUTE

Prophet/Apostle Glenn Miller has written a scholarly and spiritually insightful book. *The Prophetic Fall of the Islamic Regime* is a must read for everyone. Why? Because of the highly scriptural, revelational, and prophetic stand and views Miller addresses. It gives a proclamation and mandate establishing a Christian biblical worldview toward Islam. It exposes the diabolical duo and false thinking of many deceived Christians. It is not politically correct; it is biblically and prophetically correct! Read this book!

—Apostle John P. Kelly
President, LEAD (Leadership Education
of Apostolic Development)

In a day and age where so many voices are speaking, it is good to know that there are still prophets who can speak with clarity and authority what God is saying. Glenn Miller has proven repeatedly to be such a voice. Glenn's ministry has made an enormous impact not only on our church, but also on churches around the world. This book, *The Prophetic Fall of the Islamic Regime*, is a now word for the body of Christ, and I believe it will put in perspective the events that have caused us to suffer as a nation and will aid the Church of Jesus Christ in shaping our response that we might fulfill our God-given destiny.

—Pastor Ron Johnson
Bethel Temple
Hampton, VA

The Prophetic Fall of the Islamic Regime takes a daring look behind the curtain of current events to examine topics such as terrorism and the conflict in the Middle East. A thought-provoking exposé, the book presents an alternative perspective on contemporary issues facing our society, nation, the church, and the world at large. Miller's compelling style parallels world events with biblical prophecy and leaves the reader to draw his or her own conclusion. This book will no doubt stimulate hours of passionate debates!

—Pastors Randy and Paula White
Without Walls International Church
Tampa, FL

THE
PROPHETIC
FALL OF THE
ISLAMIC
REGIME

GLENN MILLER
with ROGER LOOMIS

CREATION
HOUSE PRESS
A STRANG COMPANY

The Prophetic Fall of the Islamic Regime
By Glenn Miller with Roger Loomis
Published by Creation House Press
A Strang Company
600 Rinehart Road
Lake Mary, Florida 32746
www.creationhouse.com

Unless otherwise noted, all Scripture quotations are from the King James Version of the Bible.

Cover design by Terry Clifton

Library of Congress Control Number: 2004112093
International Standard Book Number: 1-59185-660-4

04 05 06 07 08— 987654321
Printed in the United States of America

This book is dedicated to my wife, Sherilyn, and to my four children: Charity, Joshua, Daniel, and Joseph, who have faithfully labored with me in the ministry, for their loving support and encouragement.

This book is dedicated to the brave men and women of many nations who laid down their lives naturally and spiritually, knowingly and unknowingly, in order to accomplish God's objective to bring freedom to all mankind. Our prayers and thanks go to the families who have paid the ultimate price in this conflict so that freedom may come to so many.

Acknowledgments

So many details had to come together to develop and produce a book that adequately reflects what God is saying. Therefore, I have several people to whom I am grateful for helping make this project come to pass.

Special thanks must go to three of God's greatest prophetic voices today. My father in the Lord and mentor, Bishop Bill Hamon, who poured his life into mine for which I am eternally grateful. I am a life you have changed. Kim Clement, my dear friend whose ministry has provoked and challenged me like no other. Words to you cannot adequately express my appreciation. Sanford (Sandy) Kulkin, whose counsel, wisdom, and undying friendship have been used by God to guide and strengthen me and my family. Thank you for your ability to cause dreams to come to fruition in God.

I owe these people a debt of gratitude for participating in the vision and helping to get the message of this book out—both by way of financial support and encouraging words.

The following people facilitated the publishing of this manuscript and our ability to get this word out. Allow me to extend a very heartfelt "thank you" for the sacrifices made.

Rich and Shelly Vernon
Jim Barber
Rhonda Schmidt
Bill and Christy Miller
The Robert Bundy Family
Douglas Frano
Miriam Stevens
Richard and Rachelle Vernon
Marlene Shaffer
A & A Vinyl Destiny Worship Center First Assembly of God
Fontana Christian Fellowship International Ministries
Gates of Praise
Jesus Is Lord Living Word Christian Outreach
Michael Mauri Obrodo

Dawn Yvonne Allyn
Victor and Ixa Azar
Matthew and Janet Beard
Nan Breathitt
Tricia Brown
Pastor John Burpee
Cyril and Dalinda Campbell
Marvin and JoAnn Coleman
Ixa Corriere
LaRae Eifert
Roger and Janice Fling
Robert and Carissa Hughes
Beckey Jones
David and Glenda Langdon
Maurice and Cindy Miller
Mike and Ariann Reinmiller
Ted and Lori-Ann Uber

CONTENTS

FOREWORD

GLENN MILLER'S REVELATION in *The Prophetic Fall of the Islamic Regime* brings a desperately needed word for the Church and the world to understand what is taking place in the human race and the nations of the world.

It is absolutely necessary for the Church to understand world events from God's perspective. Prophet Miller presents a strong biblical history of God's involvement in the affairs of men and nations. It is essential that we understand the purpose that was accomplished by Jesus' coming to earth. Jesus came to demonstrate God's nature of love and mercy to mankind. His death on the cross was the singular most important event in history.

From God's purpose and perspective, it gave Him an opportunity to demonstrate His core being—that of love. Hereby, we know that God loves us in that He sent His Son to die for us. Divine love can only be demonstrated by the sacrificing of oneself for another. "Greater love hath no man than this, that a man lay down his life for his friends" (John 15:13).

One of the major reasons God created mankind as mortals with the power to reproduce like kind was so that God could begat a Son with a mortal body that could suffer, bleed, and die. Jesus fulfilled God's desire to reveal His nature of love by dying for the human race on the cross of Calvary. From man's perspective, Jesus died upon the cross to provide cleansing from sin, redemption, and the restoration of mankind to God through the lifeblood of Jesus. For the nations and wicked of the world, it gave God greater legal authority to judge every evil nation and execute His judgments upon them.

However, Jesus' dying on the cross, which revealed God's character of love, did not change God's nature as the Mighty Man of War. Jehovah God is mentioned as the Lord and God of Hosts over 280 times in the Bible. *Hosts* refers to an army, particularly one organized and poised for war.

The modern church world, by and large, does not view Jehovah God and Jesus Christ as being mighty Warriors who are personally involved in fighting mankind and demonic angelic forces. This book gives plenty of biblical examples of God's fighting against His enemies in the kingdom of wicked men and fallen angels. The nineteenth chapter of Revelation reveals Jesus as the Commander-in-Chief of a great army of holy angels and righteous saints. They make war against the rebellious nations, false religion, and Satan. Jesus and His army are victorious and ultimately cast their defeated foes into the lake of fire.

Around 600 B.C. the prophet Daniel received the revelation that four world empires would arise across the centuries. Through military conquests the next empire would take over the previous one. Historically, these four empires included the Babylonians, Persians, Greeks, and Romans. Daniel saw prophetically and wrote:

> And in the days of these kings shall the God of heaven set up a kingdom, which shall never be destroyed [the Church— the kingdom of God]: and the kingdom shall not be left to other people, but it shall break in pieces and consume all these kingdoms, and it shall stand for ever.
>
> —DANIEL 2:44

Jesus came during the time of the Roman Empire, and through His death, burial, and resurrection, birthed the Church—the kingdom of God on earth. The Church army has been given authority to execute God's will and vengeance upon the enemies of Christ. Scripture lends credence to this premise:

> Let the high praises of God be in their mouth, and two-edged sword in their hand; To execute vengeance upon the heathen, and punishments upon the people; To bind their kings with chains, and their nobles with fetters of iron; To execute upon them the judgment written: this honour have all his saints. Praise ye the LORD.
>
> —PSALM 149:6–9

Understand something. The Church-Kingdom warriors fight principalities and powers in the spiritual realm, while national soldiers fight each other in the natural realm.

I am bishop over Christian International Ministries Network, which consists of hundreds of churches, prophets, apostles, and five-fold ministers from all continents of the world. We teach that Jesus is a Warrior and we are His instruments of warfare. We practice spiritual warfare. Let me cite an example. Over 1,200 people attended our International Gathering of Apostles and Prophets Conference in 1991 when "Operation Desert Storm" was in progress.

The Lord prophetically revealed to us that the enemy had strategies that would cause 60,000 American soldiers to be killed. God challenged us to go to war in the Spirit and prevent this from happening. The Holy Spirit spoke that we were to believe, war, and destroy the plans of the enemy from working against our troops. We were responsible for saving 50,000 of the 60,000 soldiers. We prophetically warred with the high praises of God, prophetic decrees, and with all the spiritual warfare weapons given to the Church. We battled until we felt peace that we had secured life and victory for 50,000 Americans. This was proven to be a reality as details of the war and plans of the enemy were later revealed.

A few weeks later, I was ministering in a prophetic church in Tulsa, Oklahoma, when they mentioned that God had challenged them to engage in spiritual warfare for the saving of 10,000 American soldiers. I was very encouraged to find out why God told us to battle only for 50,000 troops. He had another warrior church battling for the other 10,000 soldiers! Battles are won and lost in the heavenly realm before they manifest on earth. Christians are not just sweet holy saints, but are also mighty warriors and joint heirs with Jesus Christ in His battle against evil powers, nations, and people.

Daniel prophesied that four great empires would rise and fall, one after the other, until the Church arose. His prophecy demonstrated and established the kingdom of God on earth during the first few centuries of the Church Age. During the past few centuries the Third Reich fell (under Hitler's command), the Communist empire fell, and now the Islamic empire is destined to be "broken to pieces and consumed." Daniel 2:44 prophesies their demise:

> And in the days of these kings shall the God of heaven set up a kingdom, which shall never be destroyed: and the kingdom shall not be left to other people, but it shall break in pieces and consume all these kingdoms, and it shall stand for ever.

Kingdom of God warriors are fighting the battles in the heavenly realm while America and England, along with their allies, are fighting natural battles in "Operation Iraqi Freedom" and subsequent skirmishes.

God's plans and purposes include all of His creations—mankind, spirit beings, and all the heavenly hosts. All eternal beings are intricately related in a process of God's eternal purposes being worked out.

I do not know of another book in the Christian market that gives such insight concerning God's prophetic voice to the nations. Prophet Glenn Miller dares to write what has been prophesied and even preached to the Church. He believes what he has written is a divine revelation from God. Everything he says has a biblical basis and lines up with scriptural principles and practices.

Everyone who reads with an open mind and a believing heart will be challenged to become a joint heir, colaborer, and cowarrior with Jesus Christ. We have read the account of the end result—all enemies of Christ Jesus are put under His feet, and all kingdoms of this world become the kingdom of our God and His anointed One, Jesus, and His Church!

—DR. BILL HAMON
CHAIRMAN AND FOUNDER
CHRISTIAN INTERNATIONAL MINISTRIES NETWORK
PRESIDENT, CHRISTIAN INTERNATIONAL BUSINESS NETWORK

PART I:
INTERPRETERS OF HISTORY

MY OBJECTIVES

IN THIS FIRST section, I want to illustrate the point that while news reporters deal with facts, they may at times inadvertently overlook the "real" truth behind the facts. What you read may not accurately reflect the significance of the story, not because the facts are incorrect, but because the facts alone do not reveal the unfolding objectives of the kingdom of God at work in the affairs of men.

The war in Iraq was played out in deserts and cities. News commentators did a commendable job reporting the facts; however, secular angles tend to rob God of His rightful position in the affairs of men.

Only God can accurately interpret history. This is where the prophetic voice becomes invaluable.

The prophet has always been one of the major means by which God reveals His intended purposes to His people and to the world. We must understand that history is but revelation of something God is doing in the earth, and that history is unfolding into God's ultimate purpose and objectives.

The believer in Jesus Christ understands that heaven has a vested interest in nations, events, and lives. With this in mind, we need to view the spiritual implications of the events that are now taking place in the Middle East.

Chapter 1

BEHIND THE STORY

THE UNITED STATES and her allies entered into a war with Iraq in March, 2003. Across America, protestors immediately took to the streets, staging massive anti-war demonstrations. Several nations, including France, Germany, and Turkey, along with the United Nations Security Council, refused to support America's decision to strike Iraq. President Bush received harsh criticism from several European leaders and various sectors of American society; and, of course, from both Republicans and Democrats.

As usual, some tried to reduce it to a partisan conflict. Let me remind you, *God is neither on the Republican side, nor the Democratic side. He is the side!*

This book in no way was written to serve as a political treatise. However, it is virtually impossible to not at least mention several prominent political figures and the influence they brought to this war. Their political stances certainly factored into this impending military confrontation. After all, the decision to go to war originates in the halls of government. American presidents, past and present, were called upon to make decisions. Their actions were borne out of their personal value systems, round-table discussions with cabinet members and other trusted advisors, and their perceived responsibilities to the American public and its welfare.

Wars are first fought in the minds of men before they are played out on the battlefield. Combat is strategy. The stakes are life or death. The tools of war constitute weapons of mass destruction. Our troops, led by military geniuses, included some of the finest men and women on the planet. The seen enemy in this case was a madman by the name of Saddam Hussein and his blood-thirsty regime. However, the powers that be change faces with each war. Do the names Hitler, Stalin, Mussolini, and Osama bin Laden sound familiar?

Leaders represent power, and power sides with either good or evil.

The emphasis of this book is to reveal the spiritual design and purpose behind the story. The war in Iraq was much more than a natural war. It was the result of a much greater spiritual conflict resulting in eternal repercussions, which affect over one billion souls of men. I am not minimizing the loss of our brave service personnel, who gave their lives in the Iraqi desert. Sadly, at the time of this writing, more than 900 Americans have lost their lives in this terrible conflict.

Skirmishes continue throughout Iraq. April, 2004 saw the record number of 99 service personnel killed in a single month, followed only by a November, 2003 high of 82 troops.[1] We honor their sacrifice and pray for their families.

Previous reports issued by the Department of Defense in March of 2004, one year after the war began, recorded the following statistics: the British military reported 58 deaths; Italy, 17; Spain, 8; Bulgaria, 5; Thailand, 2; Denmark, Ukraine, Estonia, and Poland reported one each.[2] Higher casualty numbers were later released for our allies, as well. The Iraqi death toll reached more than 1,050 by mid-April, 2004.[3]

In no way do I intend to debate the issues that led to this military confrontation. Needless to say, many people around the world and in America were left in confusion regarding their personal opinions about this war. One high school student was quoted as saying, "I do not believe in war at all! I believe that a country that prints 'In God We Trust' on their dollar bill should adopt non-violent tactics."[4] A wide majority, however, supported President Bush's decision. But let's face it; nobody liked the inevitability of a war with Iraq.

Why did I undertake this project?

I feel a mandate from the Throne of God to reveal the underlying reasons behind this war. Surprisingly, even many in the Church spoke out against the war. While I do not question their sincerity, I must question their interpretation of history.

Christians must interpret history from a redemptive stand-point.

Christians must embrace a biblical worldview to properly understand the major events and atrocities of history. While we are not bound by Old Testament law, we are right to embrace the basic principles of war as found in the ancient scriptures. An overview of the Old Testament absolutely and unmistakably supports the basis for war.

Accordingly, modern-day prophets are being raised up to properly interpret what God is doing in the world today. We need men today, as in the days of King David, who can rightly understand and discern the times. "And of the children of Issachar, which were men that had understanding of the times, to know what Israel ought to do" (1 Chron.12:32). That was one of the prophet's roles in Old Testament times and in today's postmodern world.

Prophets are history-breakers. They are used of God to break into history. For example, while the world watched the actions of Rome, God through the prophetic voice revealed the singular most important event of that day and hour—the Redeemer of all mankind was born in an animal stall in Bethlehem. Unless God's purpose had been revealed, the world would not have understood the strategic significance of what was taking place in the history of their day. But through the prophetic voice, man was able to take advantage of what God was doing in the earth. Without the voice of revelation, the world as a whole could not have seen or understood God's work in their day. The prophet had the ability to look beyond the natural events and see the strategic spiritual event that was unraveling.

The secular media boasts of news-breaking stories. Prophets have been reporting news-breaking stories from the beginning of time, as we know it. "Surely the Lord God will do nothing, but he revealeth his secret unto his servants the prophets" (Amos 3:7). Not unlike other conflicts, the war in Iraq was strictly covered from a secular viewpoint. However, to properly understand the significance of this conflict, we now have to look to God through

His prophets and His Word to glean a proper understanding of the spiritual significance of this conflict.

The intention of this book is not to provide a panoramic view of the events that took place in the Iraqi desert and cities. This is not a play-by-play account of battles fought and the military strategies utilized by man.

It is an account of the principles and military strategies utilized by God in war. He is the God of war!

> Who is this King of glory? The LORD strong and mighty, the LORD mighty in battle.
> —PSALM 24:8

The media, by virtue of their assignment, are supposed to give only the facts of the conflict. Given journalistic terminology, they answer the five *w*'s and the *h*. They give the *who*, the *what*, the *when*, the *where*, and the *how* of a story. From heaven's standpoint, when it comes to history, only God accurately reports on the *why*. Obviously, man has his own perspective on that, too.

Surely, you know that most of our school textbooks approach the study of history from strictly a secular point of view. This premise is understandable; but to the believer in Christ, who holds a biblical worldview, such textbooks foster misunderstandings and at times, gross compromise.

The underlying reason that historical events are distorted is due to misplaced perceptions. The Bible teaches that the natural man does not understand the things of the Spirit. "But the natural man receiveth not the things of the Spirit of God: for they are foolishness unto him: neither can he know them, because they are spiritually discerned" (1 Cor. 2:14). Only spiritually discerning eyes are able to "see" the real issues of war. These issues stem not from the faces of war, but from the spirit that drives them. Unfortunately, spiritual stories seldom make the headlines.

5

Chapter 2

VEILED IN OBSCURITY

HAD YOU READ the *Jerusalem Post* on the day Christ was crucified, His death would not have made the headlines. After all, the Romans were constantly crucifying someone. Causes around Israel, and specifically Jerusalem, were not in short supply. Some zealot, religious or not, was always trying to defy Rome.

When Jesus was born in Bethlehem, reporters would have disregarded that story as well. Had sleazy tabloids existed in Nazareth, perhaps they would have disclosed a rumor—that one of the town's engaged teenage girls was pregnant. The rumor mill would have also included something about angels appearing to several unsuspecting shepherds. Neither Rome, nor the local press, had a clue that a supernatural plan was in progress.

God has always operated in obscurity among the naturally oriented and spiritually blinded of this world. That is why the prophetic voice is so vital.

The prophetic voice reveals God's heart on any given matter. Pastor and author David Crabtree wrote, "The world that crucified Jesus was a barbaric world, a world where the life of the commoner held no value. One born in a stable, the Romans concluded, could only be an animal. As the cross was raised and tamped into place, it was just like a thousand other crucifixions on a thousand other hills. The mighty Roman Empire was just taking out its trash— nothing more, nothing less. What would it matter? He was just one peasant Jew; a bit of dust in the wind."[1]

Records for the crucified dead were non-existent. Most of them died in obscurity. They were placed in the tombs of the unknown. Surviving family members, if any, were usually given permission to claim their dead.

Crabtree continued, "Today, however, the crucifixion of the man between two thieves is remembered on every continent and in every nation. All of time looks back to a moment immediately forgotten by its executioners and forever remembered by its benefactors; the moment of ultimate grace."[2]

Some years ago a theologian summarized the death of Jesus in this manner: "Jesus was crucified on a Roman cross—this is an historical fact. Jesus died for the sins of the world—this is a theological premise. Jesus died for my sins—this is personal salvation." The historical, crucified Jesus, to the world at large, was just a good man. "For the preaching of the cross is to them that perish foolishness" (1 Cor. 1:18a). But to those of us who know Him personally, "it [the preaching of the cross] is the power of God" (v.18b).

The world at large reduced the war in Iraq to simply current events, but the sovereign God of Heaven was sending yet another message to those who had ears that could hear and eyes that could see. Again He used His prophets, the interpreters of history, to speak to both the Church and the world. Hopefully, the Church will have ears to hear what the Spirit is saying. The world will, unfortunately get the revealed and therefore real story, only after all wars have ended and redemption's story is finally and completely played out in the final battle against evil.

Remember, in God's eyes natural events are always a revelation of what is going on in the spiritual realm.

So the primary reason for the war in Iraq was not about Saddam Hussein or his regime. It was about the lying and masquerading Islamic Allah, who is a demon prince, and this false god's stranglehold over that portion of the world and all of those influenced by its lying doctrine. To focus solely on Saddam is to fall short of all of the facts. Only facts, interpreted through the eyes of a biblical worldview, speak the truth and nothing but the truth.

Chapter 3

THE ROLE OF THE PROPHET

THE BIBLE ESTABLISHES the necessity of, and gives valida-
tion for, the prophetic office in both the Old and New Testaments. Its existence is revealed from the beginning to the end of
Scripture. The Old Testament prophet provides the foundation
for understanding the prophetic ministry in the Early Church as
well as the Church of today

Prophets are represented in Scripture as very focal and key to
the plan of God. Consider some of the primary assignments of
the prophet:[1]

1. The prophet is to speak or communicate through
   declaration, writing, or an illustrated event, God's Word
   by the Spirit, primarily to His people. However, he also
   spoke to the nations and other groups or individuals
   who were not God's covenant people. This word could
   bring instruction, revelation, correction, grant assignments, comfort and encouragement, as well as bring
   conviction. In fact, the prophet was one of the main
   channels used by God to deliver a message, which carried weight and represented His authority. The prophet
   in this sense is likened to an ambassador representing
   the Throne of God.

2. Also, at times the prophet, as the Spirit revealed to him,
   predicted future events, plans, and purposes. This is the
   aspect most people attribute to the prophetic office.

3. An area not understood by many, but yet clearly
   revealed to be a major function of the prophetic office,
   is that the prophet was used by God to mature, train,

and develop God's people for their ultimate destiny and call. He carried an anointing to help the Church get into their future and destiny. Included in this function was the ability to help the Church navigate through current events and respond properly in order to fulfill God's objective and plan for that day.

4. We find prophets in the Scriptures who were kings, business leaders, political leaders, judges, priests, and elders in God's community. Often we try to put them into traditional religious mind-sets, but that was not the case then or now. The point that can be drawn from this is that their office under the prophetic mantle was far more than just giving a word from God, but it granted to them ministry right and rule, which propelled them into being focal and key influential factors in any environment that they were assigned. The anointing on their lives enabled them to leave their mark in history.

5. Another major role of the prophetic mantle was that it became a weapon in the hands of God, as illustrated by the verse in Jeremiah that his words will be a fire. God told Jeremiah, "Behold, I will make my words in thy mouth fire" (Jer. 5:14). We see this also illustrated in Jeremiah 1:10: "See, I have this day set thee over the nations and over the kingdoms, to root out, and to pull down, and to destroy, and to throw down, to build, and to plant." Jeremiah had been given a strategic assignment and authority over the nations and the kingdoms of his day. It was an effective ministry that released power to literally shake and change the nations and, thus, bring about God's ultimate purpose. God used this ministry to deal with not only the mind-sets and cultural influences of Jeremiah's day, but also as a weapon in the heavenly realm to attack demonic forces and powers that resisted the kingdom of God. This will be addressed in greater detail later.

6. Prophets were foundational and used by God to activate events in history. This function could be released on an individual, national or international scale. We see this illustrated in Ezekiel 37, where Israel is portrayed as a valley of dry bones—dead and hopeless. In every restorative work of God, when bringing Israel to a place of abundant life and purpose, the prophetic was the instrument used to bring this about. When the prophet Ezekiel prophesied as he was commanded, it activated and released a move of God into Israel.

> So I prophesied as I was commanded: and as I prophesied, there was a noise, and behold a shaking, and the bones came together, bone to his bone.
>
> And when I beheld, lo, the sinews and the flesh came up upon them, and the skin covered them above: but there was no breath in them.
>
> Then said he unto me, Prophesy unto the wind...Thus saith the Lord GOD; Come from the four winds, O breath, and breathe upon these slain, that they may live.
>
> So I prophesied as he commanded me, and the breath came into them, and they lived, and stood up upon their feet, an exceeding great army.
>
> Then he said unto me, Son of man, these bones are the whole house of Israel: behold, they say, Our bones are dried, and our hope is lost: we are cut off for our parts.
>
> Therefore prophesy and say unto them, Thus saith the Lord GOD; Behold, O my people, I will open your graves, and cause you to come up out of your graves, and bring you into the Land of Israel.
>
> And ye shall know that I am the LORD, when I have opened your graves, O my people, and brought you up out of your graves.
>
> And shall put my spirit in you, and ye shall live, and I shall place you in your own land: then shall ye know that I the LORD have spoken it, and performed it, saith the LORD.
>
> —EZEKIEL 37:7–14

7. We see, therefore, the prophet became an extension
    from the Throne of God, and his words were a vehicle
    that conveyed the very life of God and the instrument
    used by God to bring about His ultimate purpose and
    plan. Isaiah 55:11 says, "So shall my word be that goeth
    forth out of my mouth: it shall not return unto me void,
    but it shall accomplish that which I please, and it shall
    prosper in the thing whereto I sent it."

    According to Isaiah, the prophet is "the voice of him
    that crieth in the wilderness, Prepare ye the way of the
    LORD, make straight in the desert a highway for our
    God" (Isa. 40:3) We see his role again as an activator.
    It was used in a foundational capacity to launch Jesus
    into His ministry. John the Baptist WAS "the voice of
    one crying in the wilderness, Prepare ye the way of the
    Lord, make his paths straight" (Mark 1:3). Here we see
    him as an instrument attacking the entrenched reli-
    gious systems that were opposing the advent of Christ.
    He described the religious leaders not as heroes of God
    but as the "blind leading the blind" (Matt.15:14). His
    was a generation without vision, having no capacity
    to release the kingdom of God into the peoples' lives
    of their day. He literally pulled down the mountains,
    made the crooked paths straight, and exalted the
    valleys and the cultural influences of both society
    and religion to make an open door for the entrance
    of Christ. We then see his ministry influence activat-
    ing and releasing the anointing onto our Lord, as the
    heavens were opened and God gave His full approval.
    Christ's ministry was launched from that point on, and
    the year of Jubilee came.

8. Another aspect of the prophetic ministry is that it calls
    the people of God back into proper relationship and
    response to the Creator. Therefore, their words can
    carry rebuke, expose sin, proclaim righteousness, and
    warn of judgment to come. They also combat worldli-
    ness and indifference among God's people. This was the
    assignment given by God to John the Baptist:

He shall be great in the sight of the Lord, and shall drink neither wine nor strong drink; and he shall be filled with the Holy Ghost, even from his mother's womb. And many of the children of Israel shall he turn to the Lord their God. And he shall go before him in the spirit and power of Elijah, to turn the hearts of the fathers to the children, and the disobedient to the wisdom of the just; to make ready a people prepared for the Lord

—LUKE 1:15–17

9. In short, a prophet's job is to turn people to the Lord. Modern day prophets share another vitally important function with Old Testament prophets, in that they interpret history through the revelation of God. We will speak extensively on this throughout the book.

PROPHETS IN THE NEW TESTAMENT

It should be noted that in Acts, it refers to a group of prophets who traveled to Antioch from Jerusalem:

And there stood up one of them named Agabus, and signified by the Spirit that a great drought was coming upon the earth: which came to pass in the days of Claudius Caesar.

—ACTS 11:28

It should be further noted that prophets are mentioned throughout the Book of Acts and in other New Testament passages. Here are five more incidents:

1. Acts 13:1—"Now in the church that was at Antioch there were certain prophets and teachers: Barnabas, Simeon who was called Niger, Lucius of Cyrene, Manaen who had been brought up with Herod the Tetrarch, and Saul."

2. Acts 15:32—"Now Judas and Silas, themselves being prophets also, exhorted and strengthened the brethren with many words."

3. Acts 21:8-11—"On the next day we who were Paul's companions departed and came to Caesarea and entered the house of Philip the evangelist, who was one of the seven, and stayed with him. Now this man had four virgin daughters who prophesied. And as we stayed many days, a certain prophet named Agabus came down from Judea. When he had come to us, he took Paul's belt, bound his own hands and feet, and said, 'Thus says the Holy Spirit, 'So shall the Jews at Jerusalem bind the man who owns this belt, and deliver him into the hands of the Gentiles.'"

4. Corinthians 12:28—"And God has appointed these in the church: first apostles, second prophets..."

5. Ephesians 2:19–20—"Now, therefore, you are no longer strangers and foreigners, but fellow citizens with the saints and members of the household of God, having been built on the foundation of the apostles and prophets, Jesus Christ Himself being the chief cornerstone."

Why did we include this chapter, which expounds on the role of the prophet? For those who don't embrace modern-day apostles and prophets, the scriptures make it clear that the prophetic office does, in fact, operate during what we call the Church Age and/or the Age of Grace. Therefore, without apology, we submit that today's Church must embrace the five-fold gifts that Jesus placed within His Church right before He ascended to heaven, including that of prophet. The preceding references validate the office of prophet in both the Old and New Testaments. The passage of Ephesians 4:11–13 simply cannot be ignored!

And he gave some apostles; and some, prophets; and some evangelists; and some, pastors and teachers, for the perfecting of the saints, for the work of the ministry, for the edifying of the body of Christ: Till we all come in the unity of the faith, and of the knowledge of the Son of God, unto a perfect man, unto the measure of the stature of the fullness of Christ.

—EPHESIANS 4:11

13

For the sake of those who embrace the doctrine of cessation, let me reaffirm the preeminence of God's Word. Nothing takes precedence over God's revealed Word, the Bible. That acknowledgement alone gives the prophetic office the right, the authority and responsibility to prophetically address world events. By definition, Christians who embrace this cessation doctrine believe that miracles, the gifts of the Holy Spirit, the prophetic voice and all other supernatural endowments all became obsolete after the last of the original apostles died. Some go as far to say that spiritual gifts and miracles passed off the scene at the same time. Those who are committed to this viewpoint must, of necessity, find some means of understanding ministry gifts in the modern era.[2]

However, it must be noted that this cessation doctrine was never considered by the Church until the 1800's, when it was erroneously introduced by those who held fundamental theological viewpoints.[3]

Most Pentecostals and charismatic believers, who are now by far the majority in the world's Christian population, think it incredulous that God would withhold His supernatural gifts from succeeding generations of believers. Every new generation needs the saving grace of Jesus Christ, and the subsequent empowering of the Holy Spirit. And the Church most certainly needs the "job descriptions" that coincide with each judicial branch listed in Ephesians 4:11–13. Allow me to generalize (perhaps even oversimplify) the role of each:

- Apostle—to send
- Prophet—to see
- Evangelist—to tell
- Pastor—to tend
- Teacher—to teach

Remember, it is Jesus who places these wonderful gifts within His Church. All of them are needed to fulfill the Great Commission. Unfortunately, many Christians adhere to the Great Omission.

God is raising up people who will embrace full biblical precedence and doctrine so that we can fully embrace and fulfill God's purpose in this hour. For too long the traditional Church has compromised the kingdom of God by making Christianity an issue of morality—of where we go, where we do not go, and what we wear. But these concerns refer only to lifestyle issues. Biblical Christianity cannot be relegated solely to lifestyle. To be sure, Christianity will affect our lifestyle. It will cause us to change our behavior. It will bring genuine repentance; but more than that, Christianity is life. It is an all-consuming, intimate relationship with the Throne of God, to where, literally, we become the light in a dark world. And it insures our destiny as we abide in relationship with Him. We are called to bring His light to the people that so desperately need Him today. Thank God, He is raising up a fully functional Church to reveal His life and purpose to those who have a desire for Him.

Chapter 4

HISTORY IS *HIS* STORY!

Scripture reminds us:

> To every thing there is a season, and a time to every pur-
> pose under the heaven.
> —ECCLESIASTES 3:1

In Isaiah 46:9–10, the prophet tells us:

> Remember the former things of old: for I am God, and
> there is none else; I am God, and there is none like me,
> Declaring the end from the beginning, and from ancient
> times the things that are not yet done, saying, My coun-
> sel [my purpose, NIV] shall stand, and I will do all my
> pleasure.

We must come to an understanding that all of history is the
story of something God is doing. We see this clearly portrayed
in Isaiah 46:9 and 10. It is clear that God reveals Himself as the
omnipotent Master of the destinies of all men, nations, and
events. In short, God is the Lord of history.

*The message of the prophetic office is that nothing is left to
chance, but that everything has purpose. That purpose is according to a higher purpose, and that higher purpose is designed and
controlled by God. Therefore, for all Christians who understand
this concept, the focal point of their life is to seek and understand
what God wants to do and accomplish in the earth, and then work
toward fulfilling that purpose.*

History through the prophetic eye is simply an arena for the
demonstration of God's wisdom, power and glory to be revealed.

This is clearly revealed through Scripture:

> And to make all men see what is the fellowship of the mystery, which from the beginning of the world hath been hid in God, who created all things by Jesus Christ: To the intent that now unto the principalities and powers in heavenly places might be known by the church the manifold wisdom of God, According to the eternal purpose which he purposed in Christ Jesus our Lord.
>
> —EPHESIANS 3:9–11

It is clearly revealed in this passage that even though the Church is in the process of being redeemed, the Church is the instrument or theatrical presentation by which He will make known to all the principalities and powers in heavenly places the manifold wisdom of God.

By watching the unfolding history of the mortal Church and its redemption, all of creation is getting a greater revelation of both God's wisdom and purpose. If this is true for all of creation, it is certainly true that God is revealing to mankind both Himself and His purposes through our history.

Prophets today explain God's actions in light of scriptural precedents, based on revelation from the Creator.

He is a God who is moved by righteous indignation. This God, as revealed in the Bible, defies explanation.

The Book of Genesis opens with this phrase: "In the beginning God…" (Gen. 1:1). Sovereign God chose not to prove His existence or to defend His attributes. He orchestrated the creation of all things by simply speaking.

"And God said…" is recorded nine times in Chapter 1 alone. *God just is.* He identified Himself as the Creator and Sustainer of all that exists. Chapter 2 records the creation of man, and Chapter 3 describes man's fall into sin. Wonderfully, Adam's transgression did not catch our omniscient God by surprise.

By Genesis 3, He revealed His plan to redeem lost mankind. When addressing the serpent, He said:

> Because thou hast done this [deceived Eve], thou art cursed
> above all cattle, and above every beast of the field; upon thy
> belly shalt thou go, and dust shalt thou eat all the days of thy
> life. And I will put enmity between thee and the woman,
> and between thy seed and her seed; it shall bruise thy head,
> and thou shalt bruise his heel.
>
> —Genesis 3:14–15

This verse contains the first explicit promise of God's plan of redemption for the world. It predicts the ultimate victory for humankind—that of God over Satan and evil, by the prophesying of a spiritual conflict between the seed of the woman (The Lord Jesus Christ), and the seed of the serpent (Satan and his followers).

Here we have the first occurrence of the law of double reference in the scriptures. First, a visible creature is addressed, but certain statements also refer to an invisible person who is using the visible creature as a tool. Thus, two persons are involved in the same passage. The law of interpretation to follow in such passages is to associate only such statements with each individual as can refer to him. The statements of verse 14 can apply only to the serpent and not to Satan. The first part of verse 15, however, can apply to both the seed of the serpent and Satan. The last part of verse 15 can only refer to Satan and Christ.[1]

God promised that Jesus would be born of a woman, and would later be bruised through His crucifixion. Afterwards, He would be raised from the dead to completely destroy (bruise) Satan, sin and death for the sake of the human race.

We, therefore, declare these historical events not to be happenstance and indiscriminate; but all occurred exactly according to God's plan. Indeed they were revelations of the Father's heart to redeem lost man. His motivation has always been to destroy the works of the enemy.

John the Beloved picked up on this very theme when He said, "For this purpose the Son of God was manifested, that He might destroy the works of the devil" (1 John 3:8). Modern-day believers are still hearing the Master's heartbeat. These prophetic voices are sounding His clarion call.

Looking at the war in Iraq, we see it as symptomatic of an underlying problem that's been part of the make-up of the Middle East for centuries. As a matter of fact, the problem began in the Garden of Eden, which most Bible teachers believe was located somewhere between the Tigris and Euphrates Rivers, in the easternmost third of the Fertile Crescent.[2] It was in this garden where Adam and Eve fell by way of transgression; and ever since, the real enemy of our souls, not Iraq, has been on an unrelenting tirade to destroy the human race.

The Book of Daniel reveals Satan's hatred not only toward the Jews, but toward God's people in general. This master strategist tried to circumvent Daniel's understanding of end time events. Daniel 10:14 says, "Now I am come to make thee understand what shall befall thy people in the latter days: for yet the vision is for many days." Daniel received and wrote about world events that later would bring clarity and explanation to the Book of Revelation. The prophecies of Daniel and the Revelation of Jesus Christ are "twin" revelations.

Daniel, an Old Testament prophet, who lived in Babylon some twenty-seven centuries ago, experienced strong demonic resistance when praying. His experience is recorded in the Book of Daniel:

> And in the four and twentieth day of the first month, as I was by the side of the great river, which is Hiddekel; Then I lifted up mine eyes, and looked, and behold a certain man clothed in linen, whose loins were girded with fine gold of Uphaz: His body also was like the beryl, and his face as the appearance of light, and his eyes as lamps of fire, and his arms and his feet like in colour to polished brass, and the voice of his words like the voice of a multitude.
>
> —DANIEL 10:4–6

> And he said unto me, O Daniel, a man greatly beloved, understand the words that I speak unto thee, and stand upright: for unto thee am I now sent...But the prince of the kingdom of Persia withstood me one and twenty days: but, lo, Michael, one of the chief princes, came to help me...
>
> —DANIEL 10:13

19

While Daniel was fasting and praying, a spiritual battle of great magnitude was occurring. The Prince of Persia, a demon invested with great power, prevented Daniel from receiving a message from God regarding Israel's future. Because of this conflict, he had to wait twenty-one days for the revelation. This Prince of Persia was not a human king, but a demon prince from Satan's kingdom. He was defeated only when Michael, one of God's chief angels, Israel's prince (v. 21), came to Daniel's aid. This incident gives us a glimpse of then seen battles going on in the spiritual realm on our behalf.

This passage also lends credence to the idea that the nations of the world have powerful demonic principalities assigned to them to oppose the forces of God and to promote evil and ungodliness among the people.

Later, Daniel mentions the spirit prince of the kingdom of Greece. In all probability, the same principalities that ruled over Syria in Daniel's day, rule in that area today. Many Bible scholars lean toward the idea that Syria was a regional name that today would include Iran, Iraq and modern-day Syria.[3]

What Was the War in Iraq About?

First, the war in Iraq was not about oil. It was not even about Saddam Hussein and his sons. It was about a demonic power that has blinded the eyes of that section of the world for centuries. "We do not fight against flesh and blood, but against principalities, powers, against rulers of darkness, and spiritual wickedness in high places" (Eph. 6:12). Later on, I elaborate on Satan's highly systematic governmental structure. One would be hard-pressed to improve on Francis Frangipane's scholarly exegesis of this verse (chapter 12). To be sure, the enemy of our soul is a master strategist.

Today is a day of war. Jesus gives us insight into the characteristics of the times and seasons prior to His return, and He has revealed it to be a time of intense conflict. *The natural conflicts are simply a natural manifestation of spiritual events taking place in the heavens.*

In the Book of Revelation we see things taking place in the heavens—the trumpet blown, the seal removed from the book, for example. Immediately, corresponding results take place on the earth below. Also, by the statements made in Matthew 24:6–8, where Jesus responds to questions concerning end time events, we see Him tying the natural manifestations of the acceleration of war to God's purposes and plans. Therefore, the natural events are a mirror of something going on between the kingdom of God and the kingdom of darkness in the heavens.

In Matthew it states:

> And ye shall hear of wars and rumours of wars: see that ye be not troubled: for all these things must come to pass, but the end is not yet, For nation shall rise against nation, and kingdom against kingdom: and there shall be famines, and pestilences, and earthquakes, in divers places. All these are the beginning of sorrows.
>
> —MATTHEW 24:6–8

The New International Version renders verse 8 this way: "All these are the beginning of birth pains."

History, being pregnant with God's plans and purposes, has now reached the final stage prior to birth and has entered into labor. As defined by Jesus, this correlation is called the "beginning of sorrows" or "the onset of labor."

When a pregnant wife tells her husband that her labor has begun, he quickly makes ready and prepares for the birth of their child. In like manner, the body of Christ can take these signs and know God's purposes are about to be birthed, and that it is time to make ready and prepare for that which is destined to come to pass. This birth that follows will fulfill God's heart cry revealed in Numbers 14:21, " But as truly as I live, all the earth shall be filled with the glory of the Lord." What will be birthed will result in the full manifestation of God's kingdom on the earth.

Make no mistake, American and allied soldiers, along with many civilians, were killed from real bullets shot from real guns. The United States and her allies launched real missiles and dropped real bombs.

However, in the prophetic role, I am required by God to look beyond the natural weapons of warfare.

I am not a journalist. I am a prophetic voice, a man who desperately tries to hear the word of the Lord for this generation. Like other prophetic voices, I must look beyond circumstances and place what is happening in the light of redemptive history. Like you, I need "eyes to see" and "ears to hear" what the Spirit is saying.

No one can deny the tremendous role that our media plays in times of war, but they are inadequate in representing the spiritual dimensions and the intent of the Throne of God. Therefore, it is essential, that we open our ears to hear what the Spirit of God is speaking; and only by hearing can we give expression to the motivations and intentions of the only true God. And believe me, His name is not Allah! He is "The God who was, and IS and Who Is to come" (Rev. 1:8). He is the God of the Bible! He is "The way the truth and the life. No man comes unto the Father, but by Him" (John 14:6). He is Jesus, and history is His story!

Chapter 5

GOD OF WAR

HAVE YOU EVER tried to reconcile the God of the Old Testament with the Jesus of the New Testament? Jesus told His disciples, "He who has seen Me has seen the Father" (John 14:9). In John 10:30 He says, "I and the Father are one." In the gospels, we see Jesus healing the sick, showing compassion toward the multitudes, delivering the demon-possessed, feeding the poor and preaching the good news of the kingdom. At times, however, a comparative view of the Old and New Testaments reveals a not-so-benevolent God.

Do you recall the details surrounding the fall of Jericho? This incredible story is recorded in Joshua 5 and 6. All the people of Jericho were sentenced to utter destruction. The Israelites were commanded to march once around the city for six days. On the seventh day, they were commanded to march around the frightened city seven times. After completing their seventh lap, the priests were commanded to blow ram's horns.

The Bible tells us that when all of Israel shouted, the walls of the city fell and the Israelites "utterly destroyed all that was in the city, both men and women, young and old, and ox, and sheep, and ass, with the edge of the sword" (Josh. 6:21).

It is clear that God took extreme measures to bring about His purpose and plan. Unless you understand the destructive results of the powers of darkness, it seems that God was excessive. Nevertheless, His righteous plan was merciful in limiting the spread of darkness to others. Rahab was spared because of her commitment to come out of darkness and align herself with God's purposes. Just as Rahab had a change of heart through an understanding of what the God of heaven was doing in her day, so will deliverance be granted to all who align themselves with the objectives of God's kingdom in our day.

Now, let's backtrack. Before the nation of Israel entered into the Promised Land, God gave them specific and strict instructions regarding the people living there. They were to be completely destroyed.

> But of the cities of these people, which the Lord thy God doth give thee for an inheritance, thou shalt save alive nothing that breatheth: but thou shalt utterly destroy them; namely, the Hittites, and the Amorites, the Canaanites, and the Perizzites, the Hivites, and the Jebusites; as the Lord thy God hath commanded thee.
> —DEUTERONOMY 20:1–17

In other words, destroy all the "ites" in the land.

Here again, we have to look at spiritual dimensions that affect natural events. Does God hate people? Of course not! But God does hate the evil, idolatrous, and wicked spirits that deceive and control their actions. He also hates those people who have chosen to be used as instruments of darkness (See Malachi 1:3; Zechariah 8:17; Psalm 6:16; Deuteronomy 5:8–10, 7:8–10; Isaiah 10:5–6.)

God has vowed to destroy the devil's influence in the earth. The victory that Jesus secured at Calvary will one day reach its culmination when "the kingdoms of this world are become the kingdoms of our Lord, and of His Christ; and He shall reign for ever and ever" (Rev. 11:15).

The destruction of Jericho is an account about the righteous judgment of God upon a desperately wicked people. In other words, God annihilated the people of Jericho and other inhabitants of Canaan, because they had given themselves over to moral depravity and denied the one true God, Jehovah.

Archaeology reveals that the people of Canaan were involved in all kinds of idolatry, cult prostitution, violence, burning of children as sacrifices to their gods and spiritualism. The complete destruction of the Canaanites was necessary to safeguard Israel from the overwhelming influence of Canaanite culture of idolatry and sin.[1]

God knew that if the wickedness was allowed to continue, the Canaanites "would teach you…to do after all their abominations, which they have done unto their gods; so should ye sin against the Lord your God" (Deut. 20:18).

The God of the Old Testament is the God of the New Testament. However, His covenant has been empowered by the sacrifice of His Son. Jesus was the fulfillment of the covenant, thus bringing about the redemption of mankind.

Under the Old Covenant, God was working in geographical regions and with the descendents of Abraham, Isaac and Jacob. Today the ante has been raised, and God's plan is for the kingdoms of this world to become the "Kingdoms of our Lord and of His Christ" (Rev 11:15). The one thing that has not changed is His plan to bring the saving knowledge of His Son to lost mankind. God loves the whole world and all the inhabitants therein. Sadly, the Bible teaches that the "god of this world has blinded the eyes of those who believe not" (2 Cor. 4:4). However, the gods of this world will not continue to operate in open defiance of the one true God.

Just as God in the Old Testament took extreme measures to displace darkness and to bring the redemption of His kingdom to mankind, so today God is moving in just as extreme measures to bring the redemptive power of His Son to all mankind. He is still very much a God of war and is on the attack against every natural and spiritual influence that stands in the way of His plans and purposes to redeem all of mankind. The true eternal God of Creation and redemption will not be mocked!

PART II:
EXAMPLES FROM HISTORY

MY OBJECTIVES

FIRST, I WILL address the three major principles of war by which God operates. Then, we are going to travel back to ancient Egypt to apply these three principles to what happened during the spiritual tug-of-war between Moses and Pharaoh, which culminated in this heathen king's demise. I will specifically describe God's judgments in the form of ten plagues against Amenhotep II, king of ancient Egypt.

Moving along in the Old Testament, I will recount the showdown on Mount Carmel between God's prophet, Elijah, and the prophets of Baal. Again, I will demonstrate how these three principles worked in removing an ungodly king and queen. Subsequently, I will expose the false god, Allah.

In my discussions, I will not only expose these false gods, but the powers behind each.

Remember, our fight is "not against flesh and blood, but against principalities, against powers, against the rulers of the darkness of this world, against spiritual wickedness in high places" (Eph. 6:12).

Chapter 6

THREE UNDERLYING PRINCIPLES

G OD HAS A process by which He transforms the kingdoms of this world into the kingdom of His Son. We must understand this process to correctly understand the God of the Old Testament—this God of war and His actions today. When God wants to invade and change a nation, people or group from darkness to light, He will attack and judge whatever demonic powers or influences that restrict His goals. For example, the war in Iraq was not only directed to overthrow Hussein's brutal regime, but to usurp the false god, Allah. Whatever blinds the eyes of both believers and non-believers must be broken. This is true for the lost as well as Christians who are locked in bondage by ungodly spiritual restraints, keeping them from fulfilling their destiny in God.

Three major underlying principles of how God invades a society must be embraced. He must be seen as the God Who has declared war on darkness and rebellion and Who will not stop until all of the earth is filled with His glory, and, thereby, the kingdoms of this world are become the kingdom of our Lord and of His Christ.

THE THREE PRINCIPLES

1. God judges the demonic principality, power, spirit, and stronghold. Forces of darkness capture and blind a group, culture, region, or generation of those who do not believe. He will attack, and judge, and, thus, bring down demonic strongholds that oppose His righteous

kingdom. It is biblically clear that where false gods are worshiped, demonic forces are at work.

2. God begins to attack that false god, as well as those who align themselves with, represent, and propagate its spiritual influence in the earth. Accordingly Hussein *had* to go! He will judge and remove whoever represents and propagates that deceptive power.

3. God requires His people to sacrificially commit themselves to support what He is doing in the heavens and on the earth. This fulfills His judgment process. Thus, heaven and earth have to come into agreement by God's people aligning themselves with the purposes and plans of God. This requires a literal sacrifice, which we will describe later.

Just as God judged the godless Canaanites in Israel's day, the ungodly of every generation who refuse God's offer of redemption will meet their fate at the hands of our righteous God. God has not changed His mind about sin. He will tolerate no counterfeits.

Nestled among the Ten Commandments we find that our God is a jealous God and His prohibition against the worship of other gods has never been lifted.

He is the God of war, and He is rising up to do something spectacular in our day. Scripture states:

> Thou shalt not bow down thyself to them, nor serve them: for I the LORD thy God am a jealous God, visiting the iniquity of the fathers upon the children unto the third and fourth generation of them that hate me.
>
> —Exodus 20:5

Our troops not only freed the Iraqi nation from the clutches of a mad-man, but they were the instruments used by God to bring judgment and to confuse the demonic forces that were at work in the Muslim world. Interestingly, the same God who gave orders regarding the Canaanites under General Joshua in 1440 B.C., vested Himself in American military leaders in Iraq beginning in A.D. 2003. The same God who brought judgment against the Canaanites is the same God who renders judgment upon nations today. His ways are unchanging. His judgments are sure.

However, before we examine what God is doing in today's world, let's look at two Old Testament accounts that describe God's anger and corrective actions toward false gods. His decisive actions against the gods of Egypt (Exod. 7–11), along with His annihilation of the worshipers of Baal (1 Kings 18), reveal His on-going strategy against polytheism, the belief in and worship of many gods.

Both of these stories reveal God's pattern and provide us with clues as to His righteous strategies in the twenty-first century. God has an assignment and an agenda. He sits on the throne of the universe. The kingdom of God still rises up against the kingdom of darkness with the intention of taking back what rightfully belongs to the Lord God Almighty.

Jesus Christ died for the sins of the whole world, including all Muslims. Today, He is dealing decisively and powerfully with their false god, the counterfeit Allah. He has declared war, not on Iraq, but on this false deity who has blinded the eyes of and deceived over one billion Muslims worldwide.

Chapter 7

TRAVELING BACK TO ANCIENT EGYPT

CONSIDER THE LORD'S instructions and warnings found in Exodus:

> This is how you are to eat it: with your cloak tucked into your belt, your sandals on your feet and your staff in your hand. Eat it in haste; it is the LORD's Passover. On that same night I will pass through Egypt and strike down every first-born—both men and animals—and *I will bring judgment on all the gods of Egypt. I am the LORD.* The blood will be a sign for you on the houses where you are; and when I see the blood, I will pass over you. No destructive plague will touch you when I strike Egypt.
>
> —EXODUS 12:11–13, NIV, EMPHASIS ADDED

Now look at the same passage in the King James Version:

> And thus shall ye eat it; with your loins girded, your shoes on your feet, and your staff in your hand; and ye shall eat it in haste: it is the LORD's passover. For I will pass through the land of Egypt this night, and will smite all the firstborn in the land of Egypt, both man and beast; and *against all the gods of Egypt I will execute judgment: I am the LORD.* And the blood shall be to you for a token upon the houses where ye are: and when I see the blood, I will pass over you, and the plague shall not be upon you to destroy you, when I smite the land of Egypt.
>
> —EXODUS 12:11–13, KJV, EMPHASIS ADDED

To fully understand why America had to go to war with Iraq, let's travel back to ancient Egypt. Remember, where false gods manifest, demons abound. We can draw parallels from God's dealings with Pharaoh, Egypt's king, who suffered from "hardening of the heart."

> But when Pharaoh saw that there was respite, he hardened his heart, and hearkened not unto them [Moses and Aaron]; as the Lord had said.
>
> —Exodus 8:15

It is clear from Scripture that this story is a type and an example given to us for our admonition and learning. In 1 Corinthians 10:11 the Apostle Paul reminds us that "these things happened to them as examples and were written down as warnings for us, on whom the fulfillment of the ages has come" (NIV).

Through these teachings God illustrates the keys and means by which He sets the captives free.

These keys were systematically used in order to bring about Israel's deliverance and break the demonic forces or powers that enslaved His people. Exodus 1–6 describes the events that led up to the deliverance of the children of Israel from their harsh Egyptian taskmasters after four-hundred years of slavery. The exodus followed a series of judgments, or plagues, wrought through the hands of their deliverer, Moses. I will not take time to fully detail the events in Moses' life that framed his first eighty years. Suffice it to say, he received an assignment. God spoke to him from out of a burning bush.

> And the angel of the Lord appeared unto him in a flame of fire out of the midst of a bush....I am the God of thy father, the God of Abraham, the God of Isaac, and the God of Jacob....I have surely seen the affliction of my people which are in Egypt, and have heard their cry by reason of their taskmasters; for I know their sorrows; And I am come down to deliver them out of the hand of the Egyptians....Come now therefore, and I will send thee unto Pharaoh, that thou mayest bring forth my people the children of Israel out of the hands of the Egyptians.
>
> —Exodus 3:2, 6–8, 10

The assignment God gave him was to deliver the children of Israel from the clutches of a heathen king. *With every assignment from God comes the backing of heaven to fulfill that assignment.*

We must remember that God backs His assignments with His authority!

As was discussed on pages 27–28, we see the three underlying principles utilized by Moses in the process of setting God's people free.

By divine direction, the first action Moses took in fulfilling this assignment and breaking the yokes off of God's people was to confront and attack the natural and spiritual key holders of darkness over the nation. In so doing, Moses employed our principles 1 and 2. In this instance, Pharaoh represented and was aligned with the false gods, which the Egyptians worship. Moses confronted the false gods of Egypt with a series of ten plagues. Ten major demonic deities, one after another, were confronted, judged and humiliated by the one true and living God. Finally, Pharaoh's army was drowned in the sea.

It is interesting to note in Exodus 7:10 that when Aaron cast down his rod before Pharaoh, it became a serpent. In like manner, the resident magicians who were part of the government of Egypt by their enchantments turned their rods into serpents as well. Note how the Scripture is clear that the wooden rods of the Egyptians literally became snakes. This is a tremendous expression of demonic power. However, we know that Moses' serpent became the king snake and devoured the rods of the magicians. This is significant, as it represents authority. The rod was like a scepter and it represented both authority and rule.

Many have falsely thought that the idol worship in Egypt was lacking spiritual backing from demonic forces. It is clear that tremendous demonic power was wielded by the magicians to resist the move of God. At the very beginning of the assignment of Moses to release the people of Israel from Egypt, *Moses began by attacking the demonic powers and the people that represented them (Principles 1 and 2).*

The magicians were able to duplicate the first two plagues, but by the third plague they had been forced into submission and had to give glory to Jehovah as the true God. They confessed, "This is the finger of God" (Exod. 8:19).

By the sixth plague (boils; see Exodus 9:11), God's judgment fell upon the magicians and they could no longer stand. They had been adequately removed. By the ninth plague, Pharaoh is separated from Moses to see his face no more, and thus, his fate is sealed.

In Exodus 12:3–10 the third underlying principle comes into focus when God requires His people to make a lamb sacrifice and apply the blood to the door of their homes. Subsequently, God gives these specific instructions and warning:

> This is how you are to eat it: with your cloak tucked into your belt, your sandals on your feet and your staff in your hand. Eat it in haste; it is the LORD's Passover. On that same night I will pass through Egypt and strike down every first-born—both men and animals—and I will bring judgment on all the gods of Egypt. I am the LORD. The blood will be a sign for you on the houses where you are; and when I see the blood, I will pass over you. No destructive plague will touch you when I strike Egypt.
>
> —EXODUS 12:11–13, NIV

The action God required in verses 11–13 speaks volumes, in regards to the conditions that must be met by God's people in order for judgment to be fully released. One of the main requirements is that God's people must enter into full covenant. They must do so not passively, but actively working in conjunction with the Spirit of God to bring His kingdom and all its attributes to us now, thus bringing light into darkness.

The sacrifice God required in this instance was a literal sacrifice that was derived from their flocks and livelihood. It was His requirement that they participate with heaven and their substance be submitted for the purposes of heaven. This is the demonstration of our Principle 3. Of course, this sacrifice was a type and shadow of Jesus laying His life down for the sins of the whole earth and His blood setting us free from the power of death.

Our point here, however, is that Christianity without cost

is a pseudo-Christianity that does not work. True Christianity requires us taking up the cross and literally becoming a living sacrifice for the King. Not only are we bought by the blood of the Lamb, but all that we own must be submitted to become a tool for the purposes and objectives of His kingdom.

Eating the sacrifice and applying the blood to the doors of their homes spoke of consecration and coming apart from all that would defile them, and breaking all past ties to the spirits and conditions that were being judged. This, of course, meant a complete breaking away from false worship and the polytheistic thinking that was predominant in Egyptian culture at that time. All compromise had to be broken through full consecration to the Lord. No one could be involved in the darkness of the Egyptians without his fate following the same path as that of the Egyptians.

We can only judge the spirits of this age when we have chosen to have no part with them and what they do and represent.

It is clear, if we are to break the strongholds of our generation, we cannot be involved in and therefore compromised by participating in what the spirit of this world produces in our generation. Casual Christianity, through compromise, which is rampant in most of the church world, is incapable of releasing the power or anointing to break the strongholds in operation in our present time.

When we enter into consecration, and set ourselves apart holy unto the Lord, we literally become a weapon in the hand of God to pull down strongholds—not only over our lives, but geographically over where we live.

This is spoken of in Isaiah:

> The burden of Babylon, which Isaiah the son of Amoz did see. Lift ye up a banner upon the high mountain, exalt the voice unto them, shake the hand, that they may go into the gates of the nobles. I have commanded my sanctified ones, I have also called my mighty ones for mine anger, even them that rejoice in my highness. The noise of a multitude in the mountains, like as of a great people; a tumultuous noise of the kingdoms of nations gathered together: the LORD of

hosts mustereth the host of the battle. They come from far country, from the end of heaven, even the LORD, and the weapons of his indignation, to destroy the whole land.

—ISAIAH 13:1–5

Paul reminds us:

For the weapons of our warfare are not carnal, but mighty through God to the pulling down of strong holds; Casting down imaginations, and every high thing that exalteth itself against the knowledge of God, and bringing into captivity every thought to the obedience of Christ.

—2 CORINTHIANS 10:4–5

In 2 Chronicles it also speaks of consecrated acts:

If my people, which are called by my name, shall humble themselves, and pray, and seek my face, and turn from their wicked ways; then will I hear from heaven, and will forgive their sin, and will heal their land.

—2 CHRONICLES 7:14–15

Nine plagues, or judgments, were released through Moses' obedience. The tenth and final plague was released when God's people made sacrifice. The results were absolute and complete. Accordingly, God judged not some, but all the gods of Egypt and set His people free.

When the conditions set forth in these scriptures are met, we can begin to dress ourselves for our future, put shoes on our feet, get fully clothed and ready to go because something is about to happen that will open doors to our future and next level. We will have been set free from our "Egypt" and enabled to start the journey taking us to the next level of God's promise.

Many wrongly believe that our giving today is simply to supply some financial need in the church. However, in light of Scripture, we find giving is a tool that has redemptive qualities. Giving can be likened to prayer and fasting, which when used biblically and with proper motivations, release and activate God's grace into our lives. Giving that is directed by the Spirit of God can perform many functions, but that is not the scope of this book.

The area of giving that relates in this instance involves the sacrificial giving of God's people, that when directed by God, releases judgment on the enemies of God. This is revealed in Malachi 3:11, where God says "I will rebuke the devourer [Satan and his kingdom] for your sakes, and he shall not destroy the fruits of your ground." This promise is made in the context of giving.

One of the purposes of God refining or bringing the Levites to maturity was so they could bring or give offerings in righteousness. This righteous concept is explained in Malachi:

> He will sit as a refiner and purifier of silver; he will purify the Levites and refine them like gold and silver. Then the LORD will have men who will bring offerings in righteousness, and the offerings of Judah and Jerusalem will be acceptable to the LORD, as in days gone by, as in former years. So I will come near to you for judgment. I will be quick to testify against sorcerers, adulterers and perjurers, against those who defraud laborers of their wages, who oppress the widows and the fatherless, and deprive aliens of justice, but do not fear me, says the LORD Almighty.
> —MALACHI 3:3–5, NIV

When the Israelites' offerings were pleasing to the Lord (v. 4), God would send swift judgment against her enemies (verse 5). Malachi 3:3–5 clearly teaches that God judges darkness through the act of sacrifice.

It follows that God is looking for people with an understanding of how to fully utilize the weapons of warfare against darkness. Therefore, when the offering is righteous, and therefore found acceptable by the Throne of God, it is thereby turned into a weapon that will release power to break any resistance to God's plan.

Accordingly, the third principle came into play and God's power was released to bring judgment in the land of Egypt. He did this by requiring His people to enter into consecration and sacrifice through the Passover Lamb. By putting the blood on their doorposts, the Israelites were entering into a time of covenant and sacrifice with Almighty God. Their obedience broke all the remaining powers of the gods of Egypt from hindering the release of His people. The powers of darkness would be fully judged and broken.

In judging the gods of Egypt, Moses was enabled by God to act decisively by leading the people out of slavery. Finally, the God of Israel destroyed the representatives of the many false gods. Conservative Bible scholars set the date of the Exodus around 1445 B.C.[1]

We read of Pharaoh's ultimate decision and the Egyptians' imminent demise in Exodus 14: 5 and 6:

> And it was told the king of Egypt that the people fled: and the heart of Pharaoh and of his servants was turned against the people, and they said, Why have we done this, that we have let Israel go from serving us? And he made ready his chariot, and took his people with him.
>
> —EXODUS 14:5–6

Pharaoh and his army pursued the Israelites and in their arrogance, ultimately suffered total destruction because of their miscalculations. God's people were pressed up against the Red Sea with no place to go. Pharaoh, who was considered to be a god of Egypt, was blinded by his deception. He mocked the living God one time too many. We read of his demise in Exodus 14.

> And Moses stretched out his hand over the sea; and the LORD caused the sea to go back by a strong east wind all that night, and made the sea dry land, and the waters were divided. And the children of Israel went into the midst of the sea upon the dry ground: and the waters were a wall unto them on their right hand, and on their left...And the Egyptians pursued, and went in after them....And Moses stretched forth his hand over the sea, and the sea returned to his strength when the morning appeared; and the Egyptians fled against it, and the Lord overthrew the Egyptians in the midst of the sea....Thus the Lord saved Israel that day out of the hand of the Egyptians; and Israel saw the Egyptians dead upon the sea shore
>
> —EXODUS 14:21–23, 27, 30

Chapters 7–11 describe the ten plagues that tore down the fabric of Pharaoh's resolve and broke his power to control Israel. These plagues were directed as judgments toward the false gods of Egypt.

Each one was a judgment upon the idolatrous worship of a specific Egyptian deity.

God illustrated His intense disfavor toward this polytheistic nation. Remember, God is merciful, but His Holiness demands a verdict. Let's review our three premises again, before we discuss the plagues:

1. First, God first judges the principality deceiving those who do not believe.

2. Second, He removes whoever represents that deceptive power. This is the real reason we had to go to war with Iraq.

3. Third, God orchestrates an agreement between heaven and earth through the sacrifice and commitment of His people to serve heaven's purpose. This generally will be done through an offering or costly commitment. After the people come into agreement through sacrifice, judgment immediately is finalized and released.

Next, let's take a look at the ten plagues, along with the significance of each. Several Egyptian gods were decisively confronted and their influence overthrown (Principles 1 and 2).

Chapter 8

THE PLAGUES OF EGYPT

TEN PLAGUES WERE directed at Egypt. I like how Pastor Dan Betzer of Fort Myers, Florida, described them: the first three plagues were loathsome and inconvenient; the second three were painful; the third three were appalling; the final was death.[1]

Plague 1—Blood
The first plague was blood (*dahm*).[2] (See Exodus 7:14–24.) This was an attack on Hapi, the father of the gods, who was the god of the Nile River, the one who brought life-sustaining water to all of Egypt. He was responsible for watering the meadows and bringing the dew. But more important, he brought fertile inundation through the rising of the Nile. He was the male counterpart of the fertility goddess, Osiris.

The Nile was considered the link from this life to the next. It was said to flow with the blood of Osiris. The priests of Egypt held blood in abhorrence, yet they cruelly sported with the blood of the Israelites, whose children they cast into the river. The crocodile-infested waters would turn red from the blood of martyred children. The Egyptians worshiped the river, but when its waters turned to blood by the one true God, it must have reminded them of the atrocities inflicted upon the Almighty's true people. This calamity surely caused them much confusion and shame of their great god, Hapi.

Plague 2—Frogs
The second plague was frogs (*tz'fahr'day-a*).[3] (See Exodus 8:1–15.) This was an attack on Heka (*Heqt*), the toad goddess. She was the wife of Knepfh (*Khnum*), who was the goddess of the land. Also, Heka was the goddess of the resurrection and she possessed

procreative powers. Frogs were consecrated to Osiris, and were the symbol of inspiration. Frogs and toads were very sacred to the Egyptians. If someone killed a frog, even unintentionally, the offense was punishable by death.

Plague 3—Lice

The third plague was lice (*kinnim*).[4] (See Exodus 8:16–19.) This was an attack on Geb, the great cackler, who was god of the earth or vegetation. He was the father of Osiris and the husband of Nut.

Plague 4—Flies

The fourth plague was flies (*arov*).[5] (See Exodus 8:20–32.) This was an attack on Khepfi, scarab, who was the god of insects. This insect served as an emblem of Re (*Ra*), the sun god.

Plague 5—Livestock

The fifth plague was leveled against the livestock of Egypt (*dever*).[6] (See Exodus 9:1–7.) This was an attack on Apis, who was the bull god. His counterpart was Hathor, the cow goddess. Their place of worship was at On (*Heliopolis*). The Egyptians held many beasts in idolatrous veneration. The lion, wolf, dog, cat, ape, and goat were very sacred to them; but especially the ox, heifer, and ram (*Khnum*). The soul of their god Osiris was believed to reside in the body of the bull, Apis. Mnevis, the bull god, was a symbol of fertility.

Plague 6—Boils

The sixth plague was boils (*sh'chir*).[7] (See Exodus 9:8–12.) This was an attack on Thoth (*Imhotep*), who was the god of medicine. He was also the god of intelligence and wisdom. The Egyptians had several medical deities, to whom, on special occasions, they sacrificed humans. They were burned alive on a high altar. Their ashes were then cast into the air, that with every scattered ash, a blessing might descend upon the people. Moses took ashes from the furnace and cast them into the air. The ashes were scattered by the wind and descended upon all the priests, people and beasts as boils. This brought much shame to the god, Thoth.

Plague 7—Hail

The seventh plague was hail (*barad*).[8] (See Exodus 9:13–35.) This was an attack on Nut, who was the sky goddess. According to this account, hail rained down on Egypt during harvest season, the time of plenty. Like her husband, Geb, HaShem attacked and destroyed the crops. She was the mother of Osiris. Also, this was an attack on Isis, goddess of life; and Seth, the protector of crops.

Plague 8—Locusts

The eighth plague was locusts (*arbeh*).[9] (See Exodus 10:1–20.) This was an attack on Anubis, who was the god of the fields, especially cemeteries. This plague finished up the work that was begun by the hail. They devoured every herb of the land and fruit of the trees. Also, this plague was an attack on Isis, who was supposed to protect the land from swarms; and Seth, the protector of crops.

Plague 9—Darkness

The ninth plague was darkness (*choshekh*).[10] (See Exodus 10:21–29.) This was an attack on Ra or Amon-Re, the sun god. Darkness was considered to be a creation of Seth, the evil Principle destroyer of Osiris. It appeared that Re (*Ra*), the sun god, was dead, and that Seth had killed him. This plague was so terrible that the darkness could be felt. The people of Egypt wore it like a blanket. While the Egyptians were plagued by darkness, the Israelites had light. Ra is believed to be the biological father of all the Pharaohs of Egypt. Let it be said that Jehovah attacked Amon-Re and knocked his lights out! Pharaoh then was the king of all the gods.

Plague 10—Death of the Firstborn

The tenth plague brought death to the first-born, both humans and animals (*makkat b' khorot*).[11] (See Exodus 11–12.) This was an attack on Pharaoh, who was the god king. Pharaoh was considered a god, and ultimately his firstborn son would succeed him on the throne. In fact, firstborn people and animals were often worshiped. Pharaoh was considered to be the incarnation of Ra, the sun god, and Osiris, the giver of life. Because Pharaoh's son was considered to be a god, a god of Egypt actually died!

This plague was released to humble Egypt for the cruel ways they had treated God's people. Egypt had enslaved the Israelites for 400 years and had murdered her male children. The God of Israel struck back with a vengeance. His righteous anger was extended to every house that was not covered with the blood of the Passover lamb. When the death angel passed over the homes of the Israelites, and saw blood, their firstborn was spared.

> For I will pass through the land of Egypt this night, and will smite all the firstborn in the land of Egypt, both man and beast; and against all the gods of Egypt I will execute judgment: I am the Lord. And the blood shall be to you for a token upon the houses where ye are: and when I see the blood, I will pass over you, and the plague shall not be upon you, to destroy you, when I smite the land of Egypt.
> —EXODUS 12:12–13

God never takes man's rebellion against Him lightly. He will deal with it every time. Some try to evade God's call by scoffing; others simply try to ignore Him. Some tell God they can make it on their own and need no divine help. But none of these evasive tactics change the fact that this God of righteousness will have His way. The Bible describes the cycle of rebellion in Pharaoh's heart.

After Moses and his brother Aaron approached the monarch, he would relent; but when each respective plague stopped, Pharaoh would recant his promise. The Bible says he hardened his heart. Nine times, the two brothers approached Pharaoh, demanding freedom for an estimated two million Israelites. (According to the Old Testament, this figure includes 600,000 men, along with women and children). They had served long and hard in total slavery. But again and again, Pharaoh said no, and "hardened his heart, and hearkened not unto them" (Exod. 8:15).

Neither an individual nor a nation can expect to flaunt God's Word in His face without experiencing divine recompense. He is the God of retribution. "Be not deceived; God is not mocked: for whatsoever a man soweth, that shall he also reap" (Gal. 6:7). Sooner or later, God deals in a direct manner with rebellion. His reaction may come in any number of ways, but it will come. God eventually puts up roadblocks, just like He did with Pharaoh.

In Exodus 14:14, the Lord assured Moses that He would fight for Israel, but they would have to move forward toward the sea in faith.

God fights for His people as they walk in faith and obedience to His Word.

On the opposite shores of the Red Sea, with the dead Egyptians behind them, the children of Israel rose up in celebration and praise to God. Exodus 15 records a time of jubilation. Part of the "Song of Moses" says:

> The Lord is my strength and song, and He is become my salvation: He is my God, and I will prepare Him an habitation; my father's God, and I will exalt Him. The Lord is a man of war; the Lord is His name.
>
> —EXODUS 15:2–3

Pharaoh paid the ultimate price for challenging the righteous authority of Israel's God. He didn't mind if the children of Israel conducted their religious observances, just as long as they stayed in chains. He told Moses, "We will let the Hebrews worship their god, only stay in Egypt" (Exod. 8:25). What he did not understand was that God will not share His affections with other gods.

He put frogs, flies, locusts, and many other pestilences in Pharaoh's way to stop him from his headlong descent into hell. But to no avail. Pharaoh gave the Lord no choice but to lay waste the gods of Egypt (not unlike President Bush's call to arms in Iraq). Ultimately, their representative, the god of Egypt, had to be annihilated. Historically, those who oppose the righteous judgments of this Holy God meet with destruction.

Centuries later, Ahab, King of Israel, along with his demon-possessed wife, Jezebel, would come to ruin. Along with this diabolical duo, the prophets of Baal would be destroyed. Their story is told in 1 Kings. It is a terrible thing for licentious and arrogant people to fall into the hands of a just and angry God.

Do not forget. The war in Iraq was not America against Iraq. It was a confrontation between a Holy God and the principalities that controlled this Middle East nation—powers that literally threatened the welfare of the free world. This is a difficult principle to understand, especially for those who are not spiritually discerning; but then, even misunderstandings come with a price.

Chapter 9

THE DIABOLICAL DUO

SECULAR HISTORY UNCOVERS the lives and times of many famous couples. We read about them with keen interest: Anthony and Cleopatra, Napoleon and Josephine, George and Martha Washington, Abe and Mary Todd Lincoln, Bonnie and Clyde, Desi and Lucy, Charles and Diana, among others.

Biblical history also records the lives of famous couples, who made either positive or negative impacts on their generation: Adam and Eve, Abraham and Sarah, Jacob and Rebecca, Boaz and Ruth, David and Bathsheba, Job and "Mrs. Job," and Hosea and Gomer, just to name a few. The mere mention of their names elicits either good or bad responses.

You cannot separate reputation from names.

The last six chapters of 1 Kings recount the life and times of another famous couple—Ahab and Jezebel, Israel's diabolical duo. Ahab and Jezebel, by all that transpired, became the tools used by the forces of darkness. This king and queen led Israel into the worship of Baal, the chief male god and fertility god of the Canaanites.

However, Baal worship originated in Phoenicia. Baal was the "farm god" who gave increase to family and field, flocks and herds. He was likewise identified with the storm-god, Hadad, whose voice could be heard in the reverberating thunder and accompanying rain, which was necessary for the success of crops.[1]

The inhabitants of Canaan were addicted to Baal worship, which was conducted by priests in temples. In good weather, Baal rites were conducted outdoors in fields and particularly on hilltops called "high places." The cult practices included animal sacrifice, ritualistic meals and licentious dances. Near the rock altar was a sacred pillar or *massebah*. Close by was the symbol of the *asherah*, which was probably the trunk of a tree or a pillar of wood. Both of them apparently symbolized human fertility. High places included chambers for both male prostitution (*kedishim*) and sacred harlots (*kedeshoth*).[2]

The gaiety and licentious character of Baal worship always held a subtle attraction for the Hebrews, whose God bound them to a rigorous moral code. This cultic worship naturally spawned a tidal wave of sexual perversion throughout the land. Ahab and Jezebel, like most of the other kings of Israel, exercised unrestrained control. Their ungodly and immoral influence led Israel down a path of destruction.

Ahab was a pawn in the hands of Jezebel. "But there was no one like Ahab who sold himself to do wickedness in the sight of the Lord, because Jezebel stirred him up" (1 Kings 21:25). Jezebel was the daughter of Ethbaal, king of the Sidonians. When she married Ahab, she brought her religion with her to Israel. At her table were supported no less than 450 prophets of Baal and 400 prophets of his counterpart, Ashtoreth (1 Kings 18:19). She was the goddess of sensual love, maternity, and fertility. Not content with merely having Baal worship tolerated in the land of Israel, Jezebel became intolerant of true worship. The Bible says, "Jezebel massacred the prophets of the Lord" (1 Kings 18:4).

You must understand when someone is being controlled through demonic influences, such as Jezebel, he/she becomes a pawn in the hands of the enemy to directly confront and resist the kingdom of God and whosoever represents that kingdom.

Under this demonic influence, the decisions of right and wrong are no longer primary or the deciding factor of behavior. The primary motivation is getting their way or fulfilling some goal. To them the issue is no longer whether it is righteous or just—they just want their way. At this point the issues of truth, righteousness, and justice are totally secondary to a "hell-bent" motivation. When the fire at Mt. Carmel fell from Jehovah, consuming the sacrifice and proving Baal to be a false god, Jezebel was still unwilling to give up her deception and serve the one true God.

Under Jezebel's influence, those who lived by their godly

convictions also suffered. When Ahab wanted Naboth's vine-yard and offered to purchase it, Naboth would not sell because the Lord had forbidden him to sell his inheritance. Afterwards, Ahab went home and pouted to Jezebel. The wicked queen then went to work on behalf of her emasculated husband. Before that day was over, she had conscripted false witnesses to testify against Naboth. He and his family were stoned and Ahab took possession of the vineyard.

A country may very well prosper under wicked rulers, yet, as sure as it happened under Ahab and Jezebel, the righteous will suffer. Our land has, up to this time, been spared the dark cloud that wrought havoc to Christian people behind the Iron and bamboo curtains. It should be noted, however, because of godless rulers, the world at large continued to see Christians martyred during the twentieth century. Reports of persecuted and mur-dered Christians still fill the pages of our news magazines.

Tragically, not only did Saddam Hussein hate and kill Chris-tians, he also slaughtered his own people. Keeping in mind our three premises, God will judge the demonic forces that enslave His people and will remove those who represent and align them-selves with that evil influence.

Likewise, Ahab and Jezebel, the personalities behind the evil in Israel, had to be annihilated. God raised up His prophet Elijah to confront this diabolical duo. The showdown on Mount Car-mel between Elijah and the prophets of Baal makes for fascinat-ing reading.

The gunfight at the O.K. Corral in Tombstone, Arizona, in 1881, pales in comparison. In Tombstone, it was the three Earp brothers—Wyatt, Virgil and Morgan—against the Clanton gang.[3] On Mount Carmel the showdown was between God and his Prophet Elijah and the false god, Baal, and his false prophets.

From earliest times the garden, like the loveliness of Carmel, was sacred to the Canaanite Baal and other oracles. That era would come to an end on the peak of Carmel. The Earp broth-ers restored peace in lawless Tombstone. Elijah, the prophet of God, brought Israel back into allegiance to Jehovah, and slew the prophets of this foreign and false god.

Chapter 10

SHOWDOWN ON MOUNT CARMEL

CONSIDERING THE METHODS or patterns God uses when invading a culture or nation under the control of anything opposed to His plans, we must remember our three premises: He will judge the false gods which capture His people; He will remove those who propagate their influence; and this will be culminated by a sacrificial commitment and offering from God's own people, resulting in the overthrow of that darkness and the turning of people back to God.

Baal was the false god. Ahab and Jezebel, along with the false prophets, were his representatives in Israel. Both the demon god and his cohorts had to go. Elijah was given a mandate from the throne to destroy the enemies of God. We see Elijah's mandate revealed in 1 Kings:

> And it came to pass, at the time of the offering of the evening sacrifice, that Elijah the prophet came near and said, 'Lord God of Abraham, You are God in Israel and I am Your servant, and that I have done all these things at Your word." Just as Moses was sent to deliver Israel from Egypt, Elijah's mandate was to turn an apostate nation back to God. Elijah faced off with the false god, Baal. Later, he fought his prophets, Baal's representatives, and killed them all with the sword.
>
> —1 KINGS 18:36

In like manner, and unknown to most of our soldiers, the United States Armed Forces and allies were used by God to

47

continue the process of judgment in order to bring down and remove the false, masquerading god, Allah, both in Iraq and in the Muslim world at large. Removing the ungodly leaders and powers in control has opened the door for a more civilized governmental control and is initiating the removal of the barriers that would keep the gospel from reaching these people.

First Kings 18 records Elijah's second appearance before King Ahab. For three years and six months, Israel had reeled under the devastating effects of drought. The full horrors of famine, resulting in crop failures, had descended upon Samaria. Elijah, returning to Israel, found Ahab yet alive and unreformed. Queen Jezebel was still promoting the establishment of Phoenician worship on a grand scale. Baal was still deceiving the people.

Obadiah, the king's principal servant, arranged a meeting between Ahab and the prophet. The conversation began with Ahab asking Elijah, "Art thou he that troubleth Israel?" (1 Kings 18:17). Elijah answered him: "I have not troubled Israel; but thou, and thy father's house, in that ye have forsaken the commandments of the Lord, and thou hast followed Baalim" (v.18).

Elijah then challenged Ahab to a showdown in order to judge and expose Baal as a false god. He summoned an assembly to gather on Mount Carmel to once and for all end the controversy over who was the one true God. Fire was the element over which Baal was supposed to preside, so Elijah said:

> Let them therefore give us two bullocks; and let them choose one bullock for themselves, and cut it in pieces, and lay it on wood, and put no fire under: and I will dress the other bullock, and lay it on wood, and put no fire under: And call ye on the name of your gods, and I will call on the name of the Lord; and the God that answereth by fire, let him be God...
>
> —1 KINGS 18:23–24

Elijah proposed this plan to give the worshipers of Baal every advantage. What an awesome story!

On one side, we see the servant of Jehovah, along with His servant who possessed a calm demeanor. His faith was in the one true

God. On the other side, we see the prophets of Baal and Ashteroth, totaling 850, in beautifully-crafted vestments (2 Kings 10:22). They chanted vain repetitions to a false demon principality, that they called god, whose power was made impotent by Jehovah.

Their fury accelerated and their hopes dissipated as the day wore on. All day long these false prophets cried out to Baal.

They cut themselves and leaped upon the altar, mingling their blood with that of the sacrifice. But it was all to no avail. False gods cannot triumph against Jehovah.

The Bible says that Elijah began to mock the bloodied worshippers. His mockery of these false prophets revealed his fierce indignation against the immoral and cruel idolatry that Israel had embraced. His sarcasm and his uncompromising attitude expressed his unwavering loyalty to God, whom he loved and served.

> And it came to pass at noon, that Elijah mocked them, and said, Cry aloud: for he is a god; either he is talking, or he is pursuing, or he is on a journey, or peradventure he sleepeth, and must be awaked. And it came to pass, when midday was past, and they prophesied until the time of the offering of the evening sacrifice, that there was neither voice, nor any to answer, nor any that regarded.
>
> —1 KINGS 18:27–29

After gathering his onlookers, Elijah steps into our third premise, which requires an alignment and agreement between heaven and earth, through sacrifice and covenant, for the full judgment and removal of the demonic blindness over Israel. During this time in Israel there was no open worship and no offerings being given to Jehovah. To break this power, God required His representative to repair the broken altar of the Lord by building an altar, which was constructed to represent the condition of his fallen nation and their restoration.

The prophet of God built the altar with twelve stones representing the twelve tribes of Israel. He then made a trench about the altar that was large enough to contain two measures of seed. Along with that, he laid a bullock for sacrifice on the altar. Surely, doing this during a time of drought and famine would be considered precious seed and would be an extremely costly offering.

He then called for volunteers to fill four barrels with water. They were to pour the water on the burnt sacrifice and on the wood. Not one time, not two times, but three times! The sacrifice and wood were drenched and the trench was full of water. The water signified that God's Holy Spirit was about to be poured out upon all twelve tribes of Israel, thus reconciling Israel with God.

Elijah prayed a simple prayer:

> Lord God of Abraham, Isaac and of Israel, let it be known this day that thou art God in Israel, and that I am thy servant, and that I have done all these things at thy word. Hear me, O Lord, hear me, that this people may know that thou art the Lord God, and that thou hast turned their heart back again.
>
> —1 KINGS 18:36–37

The God of the impossible showed up and showed off! The fire of the Lord fell and consumed not only the sacrifice and the wood, but also the stones and the dust. It even licked up the water in the trench.

This denotes that when we align ourselves to be in covenant relationship with God and choose to be a living sacrifice, which is our reasonable service (Rom. 12:1, author's paraphrase), He will be to us a wall of fire.

In Zechariah 2:5, it says, " For I, saith the Lord, will be unto her a wall of fire round about, and will be the glory in the midst of her."

The purpose of Elijah's confrontation with the prophets of Baal was to reveal the grace of God to His people. He wanted to turn their hearts back to God (v. 37). Similarly, John the Baptist, the "Elijah" of the New Testament, had as his goal to turn the hearts of many back to God in preparation for the coming of Christ.

The spirit of Elijah is coming back into the Church and the world today. In Malachi, it states:

> Behold, I will send you Elijah the prophet before the com-
> ing of the great and dreadful day of the Lord; And he shall
> turn the heart of the fathers to the children, and the heart
> of the children to their fathers.
>
> —MALACHI 4:5–6

Just as Malachi prophesied the return of Elijah before the coming of the Lord, which has been fulfilled in part through John
the Baptist at the first coming of Jesus, so will the spirit of Elijah
be unleashed upon the Church to prepare people for the second
coming of the Lord.

We should therefore expect the modern-day prophets of God
to be use in the same manner as Elijah. Following the great showdown on Mount Carmel, *Elijah had all the prophets of Baal killed
by the sword. The evil influence had to be removed (Principles 1
and 2).* Their death sentence was just, for it was done in obedience to the Law of Moses.

In Deuteronomy, it makes it clear:

> If your very own brother, or your son or daughter, or the
> wife you love, or your closest friend secretly entices you,
> saying, "Let us go and worship other gods" (gods that nei-
> ther you nor your fathers have known, gods of the peoples
> around you, whether near or far, from one end of the land
> to the other), do not yield to him or listen to him. Show him
> no pity. Do not spare him or shield him. You must certainly
> put him to death. Your hand must be the first in putting
> him to death, and then the hands of all the people.
>
> —DEUTERONOMY 13:6–9, NIV

Many years later the prophet Jeremiah would be given similar
instructions regarding the idolatry of his day: "See I have this
day set you over the nations and over the kingdoms, to root out
and to pull down, to destroy and to throw down, to build and to
plant" (Jer. 1:10).

*Elijah's actions against the false prophets of Baal represented
God's wrath against those who were trying to destroy the faith and
spiritual heritage of His chosen people.*

His destruction of the false prophets also manifested a deep

51

concern for the people of Israel, who were being spiritually destroyed by false religions. The Apostle Paul lends credence to the idea that God's wrath will be poured out on all stubborn and unrepentant people on "the day of wrath and revelation of the righteous judgment of God" (Rom. 2:5).

John the Baptist, the forerunner of Jesus, faced off with the Pharisees and Sadducees who came to his baptism. His preaching wasn't exactly seeker friendly! His introductory remarks were, "O generation of vipers, who hath warned you to flee from the wrath to come" (Matt.3:7)?

The showdown on Mount Carmel again illustrates God's perspective toward false gods. He first attacked and judged the god involved, and then He commanded that all representatives of that god be destroyed, and that judgment was completed by an obedient sacrifice by God's people (Principles 1, 2, and 3). Although this event took place over 2,500 years ago, God still has not changed His mind about false gods. America's intervention in Iraq was not about the Iraqi people. It was not about oil. It was about principalities and powers that rule over the Middle East nations. It was an affront toward Allah, the false god of Islam.

Chapter 11

WHO IS ALLAH?
(PART I)

B EFORE WE DISCUSS this god Allah, let's take a brief look at the man who brought this god to mankind. His name was Mahomet (Mohammed). He was an Arab prophet and the founder of Islam. He was born in Mecca (Saudi Arabia) about 570 A.D. Mohammed was the son of a merchant from the ruling tribe of his day. Around the age of forty, he heard a voice telling him that he was the messenger of Allah.[1]

Subsequently, he became the prophet of a new religion. He believed that he had received by revelation, a mission to reform the world. He gathered adherents and began to attack the idolatrous religion of the Arabs. This made him unpopular, and in 622 A.D. he fled to Medina. There he was made welcome, and his erroneous doctrines made headway.

Islam would propagate yet another philosophy of life that short-circuited man's quest for salvation and failed to give real meaning to life. In his masterpiece, *Growing Strong in the Seasons of Life*, Charles Swindoll lists other philosophies that have fallen short, as well:[2]

Greece said... Be wise, know yourself.

Rome said... Be strong, discipline yourself.

Judaism says... Be holy, conform yourself.

Epicureanism says... Be sensuous, enjoy yourself.

Education says...Be resourceful, expand yourself.

Psychology says...Be confident, fulfill yourself.

Materialism says...Be acquisitive, please yourself.

Pride says...Be superior, promote yourself.

Asceticism says...Be inferior, suppress yourself.

Diplomacy says...Be reasonable, control yourself.

Communism says...Be collective, secure yourself.

Humanism says...Be capable, trust yourself.

Philanthropy says...Be unselfish, give yourself.

All of these philosophies fail to lead mankind to the one true God, personal fulfillment, and of course, salvation.

Mohammed's supposed encounters with Allah also led to a dead end in man's quest for salvation and purpose.

His revelations and teachings, recorded in the Quran, form the basis for Islam. His flight to Medina from Mecca, known as the *Hegira*, marked the beginning of the Islam era.[3]

Tradition has it that he was fleeing from his pursuers, and hid in the dark of a cave. A spider, disturbed, threw her web across the entrance, and the pursuers rushed past, with the thought that no one had entered that place, which was strung with the webs of a spider. Thereby hangs the history of centuries of Mohammedanism. One spider made the difference.[4] If this story is even remotely true, the devil used a spider's handiwork to deceive much of the world.

Mohammed's followers defeated a Meccan force in 624 A.D., but they suffered reverses in 625. Later, they repelled the Meccan siege of Medina in 627. He won control of Mecca in 632, establishing the rites of the *hajj*. He died later that year and was buried at Medina. His life, teachings, and miracles have been the subjects of Muslim devotion and reflection ever since.[5]

The god, Allah, was introduced to mankind about 600 A.D., yet Eloheem was known by the very first man who ever lived on this earth. As a matter of fact, Eloheem made Adam on the sixth day of creation in His (plural image). "And God said, Let us make man in our image, after our likeness..." (Gen. 1:26). Mohammed claimed to be a prophet, but in keeping with the Bible, his claims are rendered null and void. The Bible establishes predetermined guidelines for true prophets of God. And Allah breaks all the rules!

Here are just a few guidelines regarding true prophets:[6]

• What they say agrees with the Bible.

To the law and to the testimony: if they speak not according to this word, it is because there is no light in them.
—Isaiah 8:20

• They will have visions from the Lord.

And he said, Hear now my words. If there be a prophet among you, I the Lord will make myself known unto him in a vision, and will speak unto him in a dream.
—Numbers 12:6

• God will put *His* words in their mouth.

Then the Lord put forth his hand, and touched my mouth. And the Lord said unto me, Behold, I have put my words in thy mouth.
—Jeremiah 1:9

• They must confess that Jesus Christ came in the flesh.

Hereby know ye the Spirit of God: Every spirit that confesseth that Jesus Christ is come in the flesh is of God: and every spirit that confesseth not that Jesus Christ is come in the flesh is not of God: and this is that spirit of antichrist, whereof ye have heard that it should come; and even now already is in the world.
—1 John 4:2–3

- They exalt the one true God.

If there rise among you a prophet, or a dreamer of dreams, and giveth thee a sign or a wonder. And the sign or wonder come to pass, whereof he spake unto thee, saying, Let us go after other gods, which thou hast not known, and let us serve them; Thou shalt not hearken unto the words of that prophet, or that dreamer of dreams: for the Lord your God proveth you, to know whether you love the LORD your God with all your heart and all your soul. Ye shall walk after the LORD your God, and fear him, and keep his commandments, and obey his voice, and ye shall serve him, and cleave unto him.

—DEUTERONOMY 13:1–4

- They warn of danger.

And in those days came prophets from Jerusalem unto Antioch. And there stood up one of them named Agabus, and signified by the Spirit that there should be great dearth throughout all the world: which came to pass in the days of Claudius Caesar.

—ACTS 11:27–28

- God confirms their words.

That confirmeth the word of his servant, and performeth the counsel of his messengers; that saith to Jerusalem, Thou shalt be inhabited; and to the cities of Judah, Ye shall be built, and I will raise up the decayed places thereof.

—ISAIAH 44:26

Does Mohammed meet the above criteria for being a prophet of God? Not even close! Do you remember which day God (Eloheem) gave as a sanctified day of rest? It was the seventh day of the week. "Remember the Sabbath day, to keep it holy. Six days shalt thou labor, and do all thy work; But the seventh day is the Sabbath of the LORD thy God..." (Exod. 20:8). Mohammed named Friday as Allah's day of rest. Many rules and regulations, which supposedly Allah revealed to Mohammed, cannot be supported by the

Bible. Therefore, the only conclusion we can reach is that Mohammed is a false prophet. The god, Allah, is a false god![7]

The following article appeared in the January/February 2003 newsletter of "Saints Alive in Jesus," a California-based apologetics group, which is evangelical in nature. The group primarily generates research and study material, comparing cult groups with orthodox Christianity. The author is Ed Decker, president. He entitled it, "Islam: Another God? Another Gospel?"

> A while back I was speaking at a state university in Utah and made the statement that Mormonism was the "American Islam." I drew a comparison between the claims of Mohammed and Joseph Smith, the Koran and the Book of Mormon. During the question and answer time, I faced a number of very agitated Muslims. In fact, the Muslim interaction all but overshadowed the dialogue on Mormonism. The next day, I met with two Muslim leaders and began a series of contacts that forced me to take a deep look at its history, its tenets of belief and its comparisons to orthodox Christianity.
>
> Today, there are over seven million Muslims in the United States alone. That's more than all the Mormons, Jehovah's Witnesses and Christian Scientists combined. An extremely militant proselytizing program is under way in many major cities and in every state university I have visited. The Muslims are going to make the Mormon missionary effort look pale in comparison. As orthodox Christians, we are going to have to be ready to deal with what I believe may be the most aggressive attack on Christianity in its history.
>
> Let's take a look at the faith of Mohammed. When he was born in Mecca in 570 A.D., the black Kaaba Stone was the religious center of all Arabia. In Mohammed's day, 365 idols were worshiped there, standing in the great courtyard. One of those deities was called Allah and was the god of the Quarish tribe, of which Mohammed was a member. When the Quarish tribe took control of Mecca, all of the idols except Allah, the idol of their tribe, were destroyed.
>
> The Koran tells us that Mohammed drove the other idols

away; his god was now the only god and he was its messenger. But he kept the Kaaba as a holy, sacred place and confirmed that the black stone had the power to take away man's sins. He obligated every believer to make a pilgrimage to the stone at least once in his lifetime (Sura 22:26–37).[8]

THE SIX BELIEFS OF ISLAM

1. *God:* There is one true God, named Allah.

2. *Angels:* They are the servants of God, through whom he reveals his will. The greatest angel is Gabriel who appeared to Mohammed. Everyone has two "recording angels." One records his good deeds; the other records his bad deeds.

3. *The Prophets:* Allah has spoken through many prophets, but the final and greatest of these is Mohammed. Other prophets include Noah, Abraham, Moses, and Jesus.

4. *The Holy Books:* The Koran or Quran is the holiest book of Islam, believed to be Allah's revelation to man, and it superceded all previous revelations, including the Bible. It contains Allah's word as passed on orally to Mohammed by Gabriel. It contains 114 chapters or Suras. Muslims also recognize the Law of Moses, the Psalms, and the gospels, but consider them to be badly corrupted.

5. *The Day of Judgment:* A terrible day on which each person's good and bad deeds will be balanced to determine his fate.

6. *The Decree of God:* Allah ordains the fate of all. Muslims are fatalistic. "If Allah wills it," is the comment of a devout Muslim on almost every situation or decision he faces.[9]

THE FIVE PILLARS OF ISLAM

1. *Affirmation:* "There is no God but Allah and Mohammed is his messenger," which is recited constantly by devout Muslims.

2. *The Fast:* Faithful Muslims fast from dawn to dusk every day during the ninth month of the Islamic calendar, Ramadan, which is sacred.

3. *Almsgiving:* A worthy Muslim must give 2.5 percent of his income to the poor.

4. *Prayer:* Muslims are required to pray five times a day, kneeling and facing Mecca.

5. *The Pilgrimage:* Muslims are expected to journey to Mecca at least once in their lifetime.[10]

IS ISLAM ANOTHER GOSPEL?

Islam teaches that God is so far above men in every way that he is virtually unknowable. He will send individuals to Paradise or Hell as he chooses.[11]

Islam teaches that Jesus was a messenger of God, not the Son of God. Muslims deny that He is Almighty God come in the flesh (John 1:1–14; 1 John 4:1–2). They deny that He is divine (Col. 2:9). They deny that He died on the cross for our sins. (Most believe that Judas died in His place.) They deny that He rose from the dead (Matt. 26:28; John 19:20). They deny that He is the final, conclusive revelation of God (Heb. 1:1–2).

IS ALLAH ANOTHER GOD?

Is this stone idol the God of Abraham, Isaac, and Jacob? Just because Mohammed said so doesn't make it so! Allah chose Hagar and her son, Ishmael, for his covenant. The God of the Bible chose Abraham's other son, Isaac, as heir to His covenant (Gen. 21:12; 22:2–18).

Allah is an impersonal being, impossible to approach or comprehend. The Bible's God befriends men like Abraham (Isa. 41:8), and talks with them (Gen. 18:23)! He loved us so much He sent His only begotten Son to die for us (John 3:16)!

Allah is a god of fear and terrorism who commands destruction upon those who refuse to convert to Islam. The Bible's God delights to show His boundless mercy. His gospel is the "good news" of peace and forgiveness.

Allah requires total obedience to Islam and weighs the work of people. Allah and the Koran relegate Jesus to just the last prophet before Mohammed, below his authority. Jesus was not the way, and could only point the way to Mohammed. The Bible's God can only be reached through Jesus Christ, and trust in Him is the only way to heaven (John 14:6).

Allah required the works of Mohammed to complete his words of judgment to men. The God of the Bible sent His Son, who did the finished work of grace for men (John 19:30).

In the light of Allah's actual origin and his radical difference from the God of the Bible, we must conclude that Allah is not God. Nor is the name, Allah, a generic Middle East name for God, as even many Christians think. Allah is the name of a false god, who cannot save anyone from anything. Rather, through his false prophet, Mohammed, he continues to lead hundreds of millions into eternal darkness.[12]

In the next chapter we will take a further look into the religion of Islam and its false god. Again, we ask the question, "Who is Allah?"

Chapter 12

WHO IS ALLAH?
(PART II)

Is ALLAH GOD? Is his name just another translation for the name of God? Is the God of the Bible the Being behind the Islamic Allah? Obviously, the three principles elaborated upon in this book, call for a resounding, "No" to all the above questions.

This issue of the identity of Allah is quite disturbing indeed. So, let's get down to the basics. What are the telltale proofs regarding the true identity of two people who make similar claims? We conduct a comparative analysis of their attributes. We look at their actions, listen to their words, and gauge their attitudes. In the case of Allah vs. the God of the Bible, we look at differences in "Being," what they believe about Jesus, specifically what they espouse on Jesus and Mohammed; and very important, what they believe about the salvation of mankind.

Suppose that identical twins walk into the room where you sit. Off hand, you have a difficult time knowing who's who! They both wear the same outfit. Their hair is fixed exactly the same. Their jewelry is identical. How would you call their names correctly? You have to know their attributes! Personality differences reveal who they are. *It goes without saying that the personality of Islam's Allah collides with the personality and attributes of Almighty God as revealed in the Bible.*

Actions, words, and attitudes all speak loudly. They help us distinguish between good and bad, righteous and evil. Only God properly, and with 100 percent accuracy, discerns the motives of the heart. Allah declares himself to be God. Over one billion people on earth have been duped by his claims. The Bible declares that Jehovah is God. Who's right? The answer to this all-important question is best found in studying the attributes or nature of Allah versus the God of the Bible.

In his book on world religions, the late veteran missionary-pastor, Dr. Lester Sumrall wrote, "Muslims worship one god, and we (Christians) worship one God, but there all similarities end. Mohammed's 'god' is radically different from God as He is revealed to us by the Bible. Mohammed's god is a spiteful, selfish, autocrat who must be placated with a monotonous routine of holy motions. The God we worship is a loving, compassionate Father, Who asks only that we love Him in return."[1] Sumrall's statement reinforces our convictions on the spirit behind Islam.

So, what's the big deal? The "big deal" concerns the souls of men. If Allah is not the God of Christianity, then the eternal destiny of men is called into serious question. G. J. O. Moshay says it well in his scholarly book, *Who Is This Allah?* "In matters like these that concern the salvation of man's soul, there can be no substitute for the truth. Half-truths are dangerous. We must go deep into the Quran, Islamic traditions, history, linguistics and back to the Bible to get adequate information on this topic."[2]

To answer this question, we must in fairness and sincerity undertake a systematic study of the deity of Allah and search for the real identity of the Muslim god. Any observations must be made, not out of resentment or bitterness against Muslims, but birthed out of a love for Christ that constrains us to deal forthrightly and in love with the question at hand. To be totally righteous, we must draw our information from Muslim historians themselves, especially as contained in the Islamic traditions called the *Hadith*.

Muslims have their Quran, Christians their Bible. Perhaps the difference between the two can be found by answering the question, "Which was received and which was conceived?" This matter touches on the origins of revelation. Remember, conception is a product of man; reception is "sent down." There are contradictions between the two that cannot be overlooked!

Though Muslims claim they serve the same God as Christians, they see Christianity as the greatest threat to Islam in any land. Why? Because they have different Fathers![3]

Christians insist that Jesus is the Son of God. The Quran says, "God's curse be on them: how they are deluded away from the Truth" (Surah 9:30). Therefore, it is impossible for a Muslim to believe all the words of the Quran and still believe that Jesus is the Son of God. Islam denies His deity and reduces Him to a good prophet. Islam also rejects the Christian doctrine of the Trinity.

Again, Moshay writes, "God has indeed created man in His own image, according to the Bible. As a Trinity, He made man also a kind of trinity—spirit, soul and body—distinct, yet one. This is wonderful. If the nature of man is a mystery, how much more the nature of God?"

And without controversy great is the mystery of godliness: God was manifest in the flesh, justified in the Spirit, seen of angels, preached unto the Gentiles, believed on in the world, and received up into glory. (See 1 Timothy 3:16.)

Moshay continues, "That is the summary of the New Testament Bible. It was God that sent the angel Gabriel to announce to Mary: 'The Holy Ghost shall come upon thee, and the power of the Highest shall overshadow thee: therefore also that Holy One which shall be born of thee shall be called the Son of God' (Luke 1:35). Six-hundred and forty years later, Mohammed said an angel Gabriel came to him with a message from an Allah that Jesus was not really what the Bible says He is, and that He was just a fine prophet. The question is: which Gabriel, and whose Gabriel came to him? (He also said the Holy Spirit is the angel Gabriel. Call that a confusion if you like.)"[4]

Before Mohammed came with his message, however, the Apostle Paul had already warned:

> But though we, or an angel from heaven, preach any other gospel unto you than that which we have preached unto you, let him be accursed.
>
> —GALATIANS 1:8

The reason is that it is only an angel of the devil that can say a thing contrary to what God had already said with His own voice from heaven in the presence of many witnesses when He declared Jesus to be His Son. But Allah and his Mohammed say He cannot be, and the aspects of the Scriptures that present Jesus as the Son of God are the adulterated Scriptures. The Bible says, "Let God be true, but every man a liar" (Rom. 3:4).[5]

So, who is this Allah? We know for sure that he is not Jesus. A Muslim who accepts Jesus Christ as Lord must therefore reject his or her former religion, which explicitly denies Christ as God.

Authors Ergun Mehmet Caner and Emir Fethi Caner wrote *Unveiling Islam: An Insiders's Look at Muslim Life and Beliefs*. They pose three questions that we have already touched on—questions that touch the cornerstone of the Christian faith, and questions that beg a response. The authors often use this series of rhetorical questions to show how ridiculous it is to identify Allah with Yahweh:

- Is Allah triune? If not, then we are not talking about the same God.
- Does Allah have a Son? If not, then we are not discussing the same God. (See Surah 19:88–92.)
- Is Allah the vicarious Redeemer and atoning Lamb of God, taking away the sins of the world? If not, then we are not talking about the same God.[6]

Is Allah the God of the Bible? Strong evidence points to the contrary! The following comparisons between the beliefs of Christianity and those of Islam readily answer this question. Without a doubt, Yahweh and Allah are not one in the same Being.

Concerning their nature

- Yahweh is eternal and changeless.

Every good gift and every perfect gift is from above, and cometh down from the Father of lights, with whom is no variableness, neither shadow of turning

—JAMES 1:17

• Allah changes.

If We supersede any verse or cause it to be forgotten, We bring a better one or one similar. Do you not know that Allah has power over all things?

—SURAH 2:106

Concerning their emotions

• Yahweh loves utterly.

For God so loved the world that He gave His only begotten Son.

—JOHN 3:16

• Allah changes in affections.

If we so willed, we could have brought every soul its true guidance, but the word from me will come true: "I will fill Hell with demons and men all together."

—SURAH 32:13

Concerning their character

• Yahweh cannot lie.

In hope of eternal life, which God, that cannot lie, promised before the world began.

—TITUS 1:2

• Allah deceives.

They plot and plan, and Allah, too plans, but the best of planners [in context meaning "deceivers"] is Allah.

—SURAH 8:30

Concerning their being

• Yahweh is one God in three persons.

For in him dwelleth all the fullness of the Godhead bodily.

—COLOSSIANS 2:9

And it came to pass in those days, that Jesus came from

Nazareth of Galilee, and was baptized of John in Jordan. And straightway coming up out of the water, he saw the heavens opened, and the Spirit like a dove descending upon him: And there came a voice from heaven, saying, Thou art my beloved Son, in whom I am well pleased.

—MARK 1:9–11

• Allah can be no God but one. The Trinity is blasphemous.

They do blaspheme who say God is one of three . . . for there is no Allah except one Allah.

—SURAH 5:73

• In the one God of the Trinity are the persons of the Father, the Son, and the Holy Spirit.

Go ye therefore, and teach all nations, baptizing them in the name of the Father, and of the Son, and of the Holy Ghost.

—MATTHEW 28:19

•The Christian Trinity is three Gods—the Father, Mother (Mary), and Son (Jesus).

And behold! God will say: O Jesus the son of Mary didst say unto men, "worship me and my mother as gods" in derogation of Allah.[7]

—SURAH 5:116

Speculations abound as to Allah's real identity. Archaeologists have uncovered temples to the Moon god throughout the Middle East. From the mountains of Turkey to the banks of the Nile, the most widespread religion of the ancient world was the worship of the Moon god. Evidence suggests that Islam is nothing more than a revival of the ancient Moon-god cult. As a matter of fact, Islam has taken the symbols, the rites, the ceremonies, and even the name of its god from this pagan religion.[8]

To adequately give full treatment to the subject of Allah's true identity would require its own book. However, let me decisively state that Allah is not the God of the Bible. The preceding chart more than amply proves this premise. Allah is a false god, who overall exhibits three characteristics that more than distinguish him from the one true God. Allah is a distant sovereign, who lacks intimacy with his followers. He is a cold, calculating judge with the character of a fierce warrior. And finally, he is "the hater," whose heart is set against the infidel (*kafir*). Anyone who does not worship him must be defeated, silenced, or expelled.[9]

This was the force behind the regime of Saddam Hussein. It is no small wonder why this god had to be exposed, judged, and overthrown on Iraqi soil. Again, he who represented the god in power had to be dealt with decisively and without apology. It goes without saying that American and allied troops fought Iraqi soldiers on the ground, in caves, city and village streets, and in desert fields, and city streets. But the real enemy was unseen!

Chapter 13

THE REAL
BATTLEGROUND

THE PREMISE OF this book has been built upon the fact that the real war in Iraq, technically speaking, was not against Saddam Hussein and his regime. Although too many of our soldiers lost their lives, the war was not about the Iraqi versus American and allied troops. It was not about oil. The real war in Iraq was fought in the spiritual realm.

What many believers don't seem to understand is that Satan is a master strategist. He is not just the "bad ole' devil," as one little boy described him. He is the enemy of God and of all that is righteous, as well as every human being.

The reason he hates us is because we were created in the image of God.

Genesis 1:26 says, "And God said, "Let Us make man in our own image, after our likeness..." Man was created in the likeness of the Triune God. God's image is stamped upon us.

On the basis of this image, man could respond to and have fellowship with God. He could uniquely reflect God's love, glory, and holiness. Adam and Eve possessed a moral likeness to God, for they were sinless and holy, possessing wisdom, a heart of love, and the will to do right. They possessed a natural likeness to God. They were created personal beings with spirit, mind, emotions, self-consciousness, and the power of choice. And in one sense, man and woman's physical makeup is in God's image. God gave to human beings the image in which He was to appear visibly to them. One day the Son became "flesh and dwelt among us" (John 1:14). The writer to the Hebrews touched on this same idea: "Wherefore when he cometh into the world, he saith, Sacrifice and offering thou wouldest not, but a body hast thou prepared me." Why then, does the devil hate us? Because we "look" like God!

Once again, let me reiterate Paul's words: "For we wrestle not against flesh and blood, but against principalities, against powers, against the rulers of the darkness of this world, against spiritual wickedness in high places" (Eph. 6:12). The Christian faces spiritual conflict with Satan and a host of evil spirits. These powers of darkness are the spiritual rulers of this world who energize the ungodly, oppose God's will, and frequently attack the believers of this age. They constitute a vast multitude and are organized into a highly systematized empire of evil. The devil has clearly defined tactical maneuvers, and knows how to fight a war. And believe me, he is sinister and ruthless. His portfolio is to "kill, steal and destroy" (John 10:10). The Apostle Paul said, "...for we are not ignorant of his [Satan's] devices" (2 Cor. 2:11).

Let's look at how Satan has structured his kingdom. Author Francis Frangipane wrote an excellent book, *The Three Battlegrounds*, an in-depth view of the three arenas of spiritual warfare.[1] This masterpiece was written to equip the believer in Jesus Christ in each of the three primary battlegrounds: the mind, the Church, and the heavenly places. The book's glossary defines the four hierarchies of Satan's well-structured kingdom. One would be hard-pressed to improve on his work.

Principalities

The word *arche* means "beginning, government, or rule" and is used to describe a class of spirit-beings in the satanic hierarchy. Principalities rule over powers as well as the more numerous subcategories of demons. Principalities influence countries, regions within countries, states, cities, and even churches. These are the governmental spirits in the system of hell and are the spiritual counterpart of archangels in heaven.

They issue assignments and direct local welfare against the Church. In general, they are the administrators of evil throughout any given area.

The means through which the Church successfully wars against Principalities is through Christ's spiritual authority and the Principle of displacement. Principalities are not "cast out," for they do not dwell in people; they dwell in "heavenly places." They are displaced in the spirit-realm by the ascendancy of Christ in the Church, and through the Church, into the community.

Powers

Working with principalities, but in subjection to them, are what the Bible calls powers. The energy of a power is beamed outward from itself, broadcast like radio waves over the territory. A power is a major demonic spirit whose primary activity is to blanket a given area with energy of its particular evil. They are called powers because that is what they are—powers of darkness. They are the evil counterparts of the angelic class, virtues. A church may have a particular virtue ministering through it, such as joy or faith, the same way a power of fear or depression may minister through a degenerate section of town.

Many people during any particular week will struggle with the same unique problem. The source of this activity is often a particular power influencing an area. Instead of dealing directly with each person, binding the power over the area and then covering the people spiritually with the blood of Jesus causes the intensity of their battle to subside and victory to come.

Powers occupy a jurisdiction that is usually county-wide, although a power may frequent the mind of an influential person or build a certain negative attitude within a church. Major powers also influence the spirit realm over entire regions of countries.

Different powers will work together under the control of a principality; but usually one or two will be the most influential, eventually affecting even the mannerisms of speech in that area. An example of this would be the hard dialect of the states surrounding New York City with the slower, almost dallying language of sectors in the South.

As is the case with principalities, the means through which the Church successfully wars against powers is through the administration of Christ's spiritual authority and the principle of displacement. Powers are not "cast out." They are displaced in the spirit-realm by the fullness of the reign of Christ in the Church and through the intercessory warfare of the saints in the region.

Rulers of Darkness

When the Bible speaks of the "world rulers of darkness," it is speaking with reference to a certain class of principalities, a spiritual entity that, on a national scale, governs other principalities, as well as the powers under them. The scope a world ruler's influence is worldwide.

In the Book of Daniel, one such principality was known as the "prince over Persia." This particular world ruler fought with the angel that was sent in answer to prayer. On the natural level, Cyrus was king of Persia, but in the spirit realm there was another ruler. Daniel's intercession, you will remember, was instrumental in obtaining King Cyrus' permission for the Jews to return and rebuild Jerusalem.

In the spirit realm, however, the world ruler was resisting. Finally, Michael, who was an archangel over Israel, (equivalent to the class, world ruler), joined the original angel that was sent to Daniel and defeated the enemy. The influence of the world rulers, as well as the principalities and powers, can be observed in the differing temperaments and cultures of the European nations.

Spiritual wickedness in high places

When the Scriptures refer to heaven, they may be speaking of one of three high places, which the context of the reference interprets. The first heaven is the atmospheric heaven, the sky. "The heavens declare the glory of God; and the firmament shows His handiwork" (Ps. 19:1). The third heaven is the most familiar definition of heaven, the dwelling place of the Father. "Your kingdom come, Your will be done on earth as it is in heaven" (Matt. 6:10).

The heaven, which is the unique object of this study, is the spirit realm that immediately surrounds the consciousness of mankind. It is this realm, known frequently in the scriptures as the heavenly places, or high places, which is the battleground of our spiritual warfare. Within this realm, good and evil spirits clash in the battle for men's souls. Ultimately, when the Lord returns and all evil is banished, this heaven will be filled with the glory of God.

Frangipane writes, "Satan has legal access, given to him by God, to dwell in the domain of darkness. We must grasp this point: The devil can traffic in any area of darkness, even the darkness that still exists in a Christian's heart."[2] Isn't this food for thought?

Principalities work through personalities. Personalities influence people. And people destroy other people. The principalities over Iraq worked through Saddam Hussein, his two sons, and their close government officials and generals. They, in turn, exercised influence over the multitudes. At times, brute force and even murder were used to instill fear and gain control over the Iraqi people. Finally, the evil within had to be confronted. Allah, Islam's false god, had to be called to task.

SUMMARY

The real battleground was not the Iraqi desert, Baghdad, or any of the other cities where combat took place. The real battle, as stated before, took place in the spiritual realm above the country. The true God, Jehovah, restrained the false god Allah. Iraq was freed from the tyranny of a madman. "Operation Iraqi Freedom" drove back the enemy of enslaved and blinded men. Only history will tell to what extent. The false God of Islam, Allah, however, has been served notice.

PART III:
HISTORY IN THE MAKING

MY OBJECTIVES

In this final section, I will cover the political influences that led up to the war in Iraq, beginning with President Ronald Reagan, who was followed by two Bushes with a "thorn" in between! It is my desire to show that the hand of God in present-day history mirrors what He has done throughout history. Sometimes we miss the obvious and get entangled with secondary issues, which overshadow the primary event God is doing. Economic and governmental issues are always secondary issues in light of issues of righteousness and godly justice. Sadly enough, many Americans put being politically correct over being righteous.

Next, I would like to talk about Jesus Christ, the Son of God. He came "to seek and to save that which was lost" (Luke 19:10). That includes over one billion Muslims who live on this planet.

The Almighty's heart is breaking for the many well-meaning good Muslim people who, when they die, will be eternally banished to hell because a spirit of deception blinded them from the truth.

Jesus was more than a prophet; He is the "only begotten of the Father, full of grace and truth" (John 1:14), and thank God He died for the sins of all.

Finally, I would like to announce that God is shaking the nations of the earth and the nations are coming into alignment with God's end-time purpose. We will see the Church rise up like never before and become an end-time war machine that will do battle and push back the gates of hell, so that the captives may be set free. The largest harvest in the history of mankind is beginning to take place. This is truly an exciting time to be alive!

Chapter 14

THE FALL
OF COMMUNISM

THE FIRST ORGANIZED revolt on earth against heaven and man attempting to bypass the throne of God is recorded in Genesis 11:1–8. It is the account of the Tower of Babel. To fully understand this revolt, we must go back to the ancient beginnings of Babylon. Nimrod, which is translated "rebel," was the son of Cush and founder of the kingdom of Babylon, or the Land of Nimrod. In the Bible, Nimrod appeared as a great personality in whom earthly imperial power first appears in human history. Nimrod is represented as the establisher of Babylon (Gen.10:8–9), which is invariably outlined in Scripture, both in type and prophecy as a religiously and morally evil system.[1]

This man is described in Scriptures as "a mighty hunter before the Lord" (Gen.10:9). The simple meaning of this phrase is that Nimrod was the exact opposite of the divine ideal of a king—that of a shepherd. Whereas, a hunter gratifies himself at the expense of his victim, the shepherd expends himself for the good of his subjects. Nimrod's designation as a hunter clearly connected him with the founding of the military state based on absolute force.[2]

This same anti-God, arrogant attitude fed the driving determination of the builders who erected the Tower of Babel (Gen. 11:1–6). This ancient structure, the first of its kind, became the symbol of God—defying disobedience and pride. The original Tower of Babel was probably constructed prior to 4000 b.c.

The motivation behind its construction was to build a tower to glorify men. The sin of the people in the land of Shinar (probably modern-day Iraq) was to build a tower "whose top may reach into heaven" (v. 4). Theologians believe this tower to have been designed as a place of worship to false gods and also as an astrological tower.[3] As always, the righteous God of heaven thwarted their plans and desire to dominate the world and their own destiny. He short-circuited their man-centered organizational unity, power, and great accomplishments. Their common belief was that having all things in common and moving in one direction, man could save himself by his own efforts. Their purpose was fueled by pride and rebellion against God. And God, as usual, shut down their intentions. Confusing the languages of the builders halted the construction of this massive undertaking.

When judgment fell and God overthrew that darkness, immediately it opened doors for God to bring light where darkness had been. In Genesis 12, this was carried out by God through the call of a man from that same area, Abram, whose name was later changed to Abraham, the Father of many nations.

This very same spirit raised its ugly head again in the beginning of the twentieth century through the rise of Communism.

Inherent in Communism were many of the same traits that we find at the Tower of Babel. Under this system, ideally, everyone had all things in common. Religion was considered the opiate of the masses and God was no longer needed nor believed in. Christians were persecuted. The system was based on humanistic principles and man saving himself.

God raised up President Ronald Reagan with an assignment to do war against Communism. President Reagan defined the Soviet Union and those aligned with it as an evil empire. Whether President Reagan was aware or understood there were spiritual implications to his actions, I do not know. As the leader of the free world, he initiated economic and political pressures on the Communist Block, exposed its weaknesses and caused its downfall.

He was the Lord's anointed and appointed one to bring about judgment on this darkness. He even called for Mikhail Gorbachev to tear down the Iron Curtain. Just like at the Tower of Babel, Communism was brought down without a single shot being fired. God divided their ranks and subsequently the barriers to the gospel were broken and the greatest revival in that part of the world immediately began to take place.

When God invades a culture, He will break off the darkness so that He can bring the light of the saving grace of His Son.

Subsequent American presidents were issued assignments from the Throne of God, as well. Let's see how they handled or mishandled their God-given mandates.

Chapter 15

THE "THORN" BETWEEN
TWO BUSHES

SINCE 1989, TWO men with the last name of Bush have appeared on the national and international scene. This father and son not only shared last names, they shared similar mandates. Both were given the assignment to face off with Iraqi tyrant, Saddam Hussein.

Our forty-first president, George Herbert Walker Bush, made contributions both in time of war and in peace. On his eighteenth birthday he enlisted in the Armed Forces. He was the youngest pilot in the Navy when he received his wings; he flew fifty-eight combat missions during World War II. In 1980 Bush campaigned for the Republican nomination for president. He lost, but was chosen as a running mate by Ronald Reagan.[1]

As vice president, Bush had responsibility in several domestic areas, including federal deregulation and anti-drug programs, and visited scores of foreign countries. In 1988 Bush won the Republican nomination for president and, with Senator Dan Quayle of Indiana as his running mate, he defeated Massachusetts Governor Michael Dukakis in the general election.[2]

Bush faced a dramatically changing world, as the Cold War ended after forty bitter years, the Communist Empire broke up and the Berlin Wall fell. The Soviet Union ceased to exist; and reformist President Mikhail Gorbachev, whom Bush had supported, resigned. While Bush hailed the march of democracy, he insisted on restraint in U.S. policy toward the new group of nations.

In other areas of foreign policy, President Bush sent American troops into Panama to overthrow the corrupt regime of General

Manuel Noriega, who was threatening the security of the canal and the Americans living there. Noriega was brought to the United States for trial as a drug trafficker.

Bush's greatest test, however, came when Iraqi president, Saddam Hussein, invaded Kuwait, and then threatened to move into Saudi Arabia. Vowing to free Kuwait, Bush rallied the United Nations, the American people, and Congress and sent 425,000 American troops. They were joined by 118,000 troops from allied nations. After weeks of air and missile bombardments, the one-hundred-hour land battle dubbed "Desert Storm" routed Iraq's million-man army.[3] Do you remember where you were and what you were doing when "Operation Desert Storm" was launched in January of 1991?

However, I believe that George H. W. Bush fell short of his mandate. Why? Recall the three premises of how God invades a culture. He will judge the spirit that is holding the people captive; He will remove whoever represents and aligns with that demonic power; and then call for a sacrificial alignment by God's people with God's purpose.

Unfortunately, Mr. Bush allowed the international community and the fear of wide-scale casualties to back him down in the day of battle. President Bush started the process; however, he failed to remove the man. His unwillingness to pay the full price resulted in his not fulfilling his God-given objective. Being ignorant to the spiritual ramifications of his actions, public opinion would declare him successful. It is my conviction that he quit short of completing his godly assignment. His primary assignment was to remove Saddam Hussein from control in Iraq.

Instead, the first Bush turned back in the day of conquest and let this tyrant live. It was a mistake, a great mistake. As a result, Saddam Hussein claimed he had a great victory and openly gave praise to Allah. *The judgment process was thwarted on all three premises because none of the premises had been completely met.*

God wanted to start the process of judgment to bring down the false god Allah in 1991; however, the first President Bush stopped short of a military push into the seat of power of Iraqi in Baghdad. Our service personnel came back home in record time, and America applauded the first President Bush. At that time he received the highest ratings of presidential approval ever recorded. However, I believe God rejected him as a leader, because he did not complete his whole assignment. Iraq remained in the clutches of a madman. The first President Bush lost his bid for re-election in 1992 to Democrat William Clinton.

George H. W. Bush's presidency can be likened to events in Saul's life, the first king of Israel.

He, too, stopped short of completing an assignment based on his fear of public opinion. In 1 Samuel 15:24, it says, "And Saul said unto Samuel, I have sinned: for I have transgressed the commandment of the Lord, and thy words: because I feared the people, and obeyed their voice."

This entire story is found in 1 Samuel 15. Saul directly disobeyed his commission from God through the prophet Samuel to utterly destroy the Amalekites. Note these excerpts:

> Samuel also said unto Saul, the LORD sent me to anoint thee to be king over his people, over Israel: now therefore hearken thou unto the voice of the LORD. Thus saith the LORD of hosts, I remember that which Amalek did to Israel, how he laid wait for him in the way, when he came up from Egypt. Now go and smite Amalek, and utterly destroy all that they have, and spare them not. But Saul and the people spared Agag, and the best of the sheep, and of the oxen, and of the fatlings, and the lambs, and all that was good.
>
> —1 SAMUEL 1–3, 9

The Amalekites had been the first to oppose God and the nation of Israel in the wilderness. They represented all evil power and opposition to God, His people, and the truth. It was Saul's responsibility to completely destroy the Amalekites and their evil ways. Hiding behind a cloak of religious zeal, however, he refused to obey the Lord's command:

"Now go and smite Amalek, and utterly destroy all that they have…" (1 Sam. 15:3). As a result of Saul's disobedience, he was rejected by God. " It repenteth me that I have set up Saul to be king: for he is turned back from following me, and hath not performed my commandments" (1 Sam. 15:11). Later, God would reject him as king altogether. "Because thou hast rejected the word of the Lord, he hath also rejected thee from being king" (1 Sam. 15:23).

President George H. W. Bush missed fulfilling his complete destiny by pulling back in the day of battle. He turned back and allowed a man God marked for death to remain alive. He let Saddam Hussein live. This is a foreign concept to many. It sounds ruthless to others. But God's people must get that type of humanistic nonsense out of their heads and look at the bigger picture.

They argued that people would get hurt and die, but the bigger picture was that if we didn't go to war, many more people would die, and, tragically, many more would go to hell and die forever. It is always God's mercy to break down barriers that keep people from the saving knowledge of His Son. It was a time of war. It was time to blow the trumpet in Zion. Face it. Saddam Hussein represented a false god. He was empowered by demons. He was backed by a false god. Jehovah had to do battle against this false god. You do not think Saddam was waiting to repent and acknowledge Jesus Christ as Savior and Lord, do you?

We must get beyond our limited mindsets to see what's really going on. Jehovah is still on the Throne! He brings down nations and lifts up nations to accomplish His purposes in the earth.

What am I saying? I am heralding the prophetic voice. I am not attacking our forty-first president, as I believe he was a godly man. I am looking at what he did and did not do in light of redemptive history. However, I must commend him for having a godly lifestyle and the parenting skills necessary to impart godly virtues and character into his son, thereby enabling his son to complete the tasks his own administration left undone. So, when giving credit to the second President Bush, we cannot forget the contributions of the first President Bush. In the end, the second President Bush was able to start where the first President Bush left off. Every parent's desire should be that their children go where they themselves could only dream to go.

THE "THORN"

George H. W. Bush left office in 1993, when William Jefferson Clinton became our forty-second President. About a week before the election of 1992, I felt impressed of the Lord that Mr. Clinton would be our next commander in chief. I was so heart-broken, not because I had a personal vendetta against the man, but because I hated much of what he represented. His election as president said something about the American public that was not good.

The Lord spoke to me in my anguish and said, "My people have rejected Me. As a result, protective hedges that have been in place in America from her beginning days will begin to come down." It came as no surprise to me that examination of the exit polling revealed that Clinton won only because the Christian vote that had put Presidents Reagan and Bush into office had split under Clinton.

Before President Clinton's inauguration, I felt the Lord speak to me that there were two major consequences that would impact our society as a result of this election. Subsequently, I preached and prophesied in churches throughout America regarding these two things:

1. Terrorism will come to the shores of America like never before.

2. Perversion will explode in America.

Many of God's people voted for a candidate based on reasons of prosperity, rather than issues of righteousness.

Without argument, during Clinton's administration the U.S. enjoyed much peace and economic well-being. He was the first Democratic president since Franklin D. Roosevelt to win a second term. He could point to the lowest unemployment rate in modern times, the lowest inflation in thirty years, the highest home ownership in the country's history, dropping crime rates in many places, and reduced welfare roles. He proposed the first balanced budget in decades and achieved a budget surplus.[4] Naturally speaking, his performance looked commendable.

However, Jehovah God places a premium on righteous living, and promises His people provision and help if they place their priorities in His kingdom: "Seek ye first the kingdom of God and

His righteousness, and all these things shall be added unto you" (Matt. 6:33). The psalmist concurred when he said, "Better is one day in your courts than a thousand elsewhere; I would rather be a doorkeeper in the house of my God than dwell in the tents of the wicked" (Ps. 84:10, niv).

God places a higher premium on personal lifestyle than He does on economics. In Psalm 84:11, it says, "For the Lord God is a sun and shield; the Lord bestows favor and honor; no good thing does he withhold from those whose walk is blameless." This promise is specifically directed to believers who sincerely endeavor to live godly and righteous lives. What God regards as good relates directly to our fulfilling His purpose for our lives. Be careful about your lifestyle.

The way you live literally determines your destiny!

WORSHIPING AT THE ALTAR OF MOLECH

Since 1973, over thirty-five million babies in America have been sacrificed on the altar of Molech. This detestable Semitic deity was honored by sacrificing children who were forced to pass through fire. Palestinian excavations have uncovered infant skeletal remains in burial places around heathen shrines. These ungodly acts were performed by parents who were not willing to have their lives encumbered by offspring. This shedding of innocent blood was selfishness personified. In most cases, at least one child was sacrificed per family by the age of two.[5]

Today, the killing has shifted to those yet unborn. We have assigned a new name to this most selfish act: Abortion.

Obviously, abortion was legalized in America long before President Clinton went into office. However, during his presidency, we were just one vote away from overturning Roe vs. Wade. He appointed Supreme Court justices who were openly pro-choice.

The worship of Molech continues to this day in America. Last year alone, hundreds of thousands of babies were sacrificed to this god in the abortion mills of our nation. This is the same nation that uses tax dollars to "save the whales."

Leaders who allow such atrocities bare the responsibilities

before a holy God. Their hands are as bloody as Hitler's hands. Six million Jews went to their death under the direct orders of this twentieth century madman. God hates the shedding of innocent blood. As a matter of fact, it is one of seven sins listed in Proverbs 6. "These six things doth the Lord hate: yea, seven are an abomination unto Him...hands that shed innocent blood..." (vv. 16–17).

In 1998, as a result of issues surrounding personal indiscretions with a young White House intern, Clinton was the second U.S. President to be impeached by the House of Representatives. He was tried in the Senate and found not guilty of the charges brought against him by a narrow margin. He later apologized to the nation and continued to have unprecedented popular approval ratings for his performance as president.[6]

The phrase "politically correct" began to accelerate; thus justifying the president's actions to a nation that has progressively embraced relativism over moral absolutes.

Relativism strips individuals of personal responsibility and accountability and places personal rights on the throne of their lives.

Right and wrong is reduced to "what works for me." Individuals become their own plumb line. The "I am a god" belief feeds into gross "me-ism," a philosophy that puts my personal values and interests on the throne of my life.

When you dethrone the King, the true and living God, you open yourself up to trouble. Judges 21:25 says, "In those days there was no king in Israel, every man did that which was right in his own eyes." During the time judges ruled Israel, the Israelites ignored God's standards for them and did what was right in their own judgment. But two identical Proverbs point out that human thoughts and opinions are a poor gauge of what is right. Both Proverbs 14:12 and 16:25 say, "There is a way which seemeth right unto a man, but the end thereof are the ways of death." To make our opinions the guide for our lives rather than God's Word is nothing less than rebellion against God.

On the world scene, Mr. Clinton successfully dispatched peace-keeping forces to war-torn Bosnia and bombed Iraq when Saddam Hussein stopped United Nations inspections for evidence of nuclear, chemical and biological weapons.[7] Like his predecessor, Clinton clearly did not understand the true nature of this "killing machine."

Hussein would remain as leader of Iraq for the next Bush to confront.

The Bible says, "That righteousness exalts a nation, but sin is a reproach to any people" (Prov. 14:34). The term "alternate life-style" was coined by those who stood against the biblical norm regarding heterosexual relationships. As moral absolutes continued to erode, more and more Americans began to embrace the "If it feels good, do it" mentality. Mr. Clinton openly supported gay rights and took issue with the military's long-held standard regarding the dishonorable discharge of admitted homosexuals serving in the Armed Forces.

For too long, evangelicals have been accused of hating those bound in the gay lifestyle. Unfortunately, some misguided Christians have mishandled certain situations; but the truth remains— God has called us to hate the sin and love the sinner. The open acceptance of the homosexual lifestyle is an abomination to God. Leviticus 18:22 makes this clear. Verses 24 and 25a issue this command and warning: "Defile not ye yourselves in any of these things: for in all these the nations are defiled which I cast out before you: And the land is defiled..."

It is a historical fact that whenever a nation disregards moral absolutes, that nation quickly spirals downwardly and begins to rot from the inside out. It literally self-destructs. The Ten Commandments were never presented as "The Ten Suggestions." God made us, and He established parameters that would keep us healthy—physically, emotionally, and spiritually. These ancient commandments are not obsolete; they provide humanity with wonderful boundaries for maintaining self-preservation. History supports this presupposition.

In great part, the disintegration of the Roman Empire was due to the moral landslide that occurred, much of it generated by the empire's rulers. The noted historian, Edward Gibbons, who wrote *The Rise and Fall of the Roman Empire*, gave five reasons for the fall of the great dynasty. The fifth reason he cited was the acceptance of sexual immorality—more specifically, homosexuality.[8] What was once considered an invincible empire fell to the Byzantine Empire, due to internal rot.

Modern-day signs in America, sadly enough, parallel the Roman Empire's internal demise. One government study conducted in the early 1990s revealed that 1.5 percent of the American population was admittedly homosexual. An Associated Press study based on a 1994 survey reported, "Same-sex attraction called high—up to 20 percent in United States 'incidentally gay.'" This percentage exploded during the Clinton years.[9] It makes sense that leaders who embrace the dissolution of absolutes, grant immoral license to the masses.

Meanwhile, the phrase *bipopulation* was used to describe a growing trend toward the acceptance of bisexuality. Some dubbed them the "try population," as it seemed that many Americans were adopting an "if it feels good, try it" philosophy of life. A move toward hedonistic thinking, or the love of pleasure, infiltrated not only the halls of government but manifested in the school halls. School textbooks became the battleground for same-sex proponents versus those who held tightly to the ideals of heterosexual monogamy. The Apostle Paul's description of lifestyles in the last days came into focus: "This know also, that in the last days perilous times shall come. For men shall be...lovers of pleasure more than lovers of God..." (2 Tim. 3:1–2, 4).

During these same years, incidences of gay bashing fostered national media attention. Certainly, two wrongs don't make one right, as reports of stalking and even the murdering of alleged gays filled the nation's evening newscasts. One highly publicized case was that of Matthew Shephard in October, 1998.

According to one Human Rights Campaign news release, "Shephard, 21, a student from the University of Wyoming was savagely attacked, burned and left to die...tied to a wooden fence post outside Laramie, 30 miles northwest of Cheyenne, (Wyoming)."[10] Later, this tragic story would be featured in a made-for-television movie.

A major paradigm shift accelerated in America during the 1990s. Its roots could be traced back as far as the 1920s, to what historians refer to as "The Roaring Twenties." You see, internal decay does not happen overnight.

A paradigm shift is defined as changing trends in the way people think, or the lenses through which they view life.

Our perspective, or the way we view things, hinges on our value system. The believer in Jesus Christ adheres to God's Word, the Bible, and bases his belief system upon its infallible truths.

As the decades of the twentieth century wore on in America, it seemed various sectors of society began to express disdain toward its Judeo-Christian heritage. Post-moderns, as they were contemporarily described, began to embrace pluralistic thinking. A large segment rejected the necessity of living according to moral absolutes. These shifts away from traditional Judeo-Christian values were at first slow, but steady. However, the past forty-plus years in America have seen an acceleration of anti-biblical values that have found unrestrained public expression.

Public conscience has seemed to more easily tolerate a move from conservative values to a more liberal agenda. Incredibly, pornography grew to a multi-billion dollar industry, and Hollywood continued to use sex to sell everything from microwave dinners to cars. Certainly, perversion has exploded in America.

When President Clinton left office in January 2001, the American people were divided in their values. Statistics tell the story. The election of 2000 indicated that 50 percent of American voters continued to place a higher premium on the economy over righteous living. George W. Bush won this strategic election over his Democratic opponent Albert Gore by a narrow margin of only 537 votes. Mr. Bush had an assignment from above!

THE OTHER BUSH

George W. Bush was inaugurated as the forty-third president of the United States on January 20, 2001. However, on election night, America held its collective breath, as the final count in Florida looked too close to call. Al Gore, his Democratic opponent, conceded the election, but later rescinded his concession when a counting discrepancy was announced. After five weeks of complicated legal battles that stretched all the way to the highest court in the land, the United States Supreme Court ruled five-to-four to stop the recounts. Bush was declared the winner by a margin of 537 votes.

George W. Bush, I believe, was God's choice. God anointed him. He came into the presidency for such a time as this. My good friend, Kim Clement, who is one of the most respected and greatest prophets of our day, prophesied before the election that God was going to place a "burning Bush" in the White House.

Before the inauguration of the second President Bush, I prophesied to many people, including many Christian leaders, that George W. Bush would be going to Iraq to finish what his father had left undone. It is my conviction God gave him a mandate from the Throne, and his assignment was to drive out Saddam Hussein.

Why did we have to go to war? God wanted to crush the power of the false god who was oppressing this ancient people.

He used George Bush to accomplish His sovereign purpose. What Moses was to Pharaoh, what Elijah was to Ahab and Jezebel, George Bush was to Saddam Hussein. The king of Egypt, the "diabolical duo," and the dictator of Iraq were all controlled by false gods and more specifically, demons.

Some in the Church are pronouncing gloom and doom upon America, but I believe that God has plans for our country and the greatest days of America are in her future. She will continue to be an instrument in the hand of Almighty God. We are still "One nation under God."

Does this mean we are a Christian nation? That is questionable. However, there are still enough God-fearing, praying believers in this country to help stem the tide of world events. If God could use a faithful remnant, including Daniel, in ancient Babylon, He can and will use a praying remnant today. In Jesus' name, we need peace, but we need peace that is a righteous peace.

Let me give further explanation as to why I believe George W. Bush is the Lord's anointed. First, he was raised up by God to complete an assignment—to drive out Allah's representative in Iraq. Second, he testified to a born-again experience in July of 1986. In response to questions from reporters about possible drug use and heavy drinking during his bachelor days in Midland, Texas, Bush has called the early 1970s his "nomadic period."

However, shortly after his fortieth birthday, the sometimes wayward Bush reached a turning point in his personal and professional life. He quit drinking altogether and became more religious, turning to his wife's Methodist faith.[11] This is the media's way of saying that he placed his faith in the saving grace of Jesus Christ.

Following the terrorist attacks of September 11, 2001, Bush declared a war against terrorism, marking the rise of a unilateral and muscular approach to U.S. foreign policy. In 2002, after a lapse of four years, the United Nations resumed weapons inspections in Iraq, warning serious consequences if Saddam Hussein failed to offer inspectors unrestricted access. Almost immediately after the U.N. resolution was passed, diplomats started disagreeing on whether the use of force was justified if Iraq did not comply.[12]

In March of 2003, after months of debate, the United States and Britain led the war on Iraq without the support of the U.N. Security Council. After four weeks, coalition ground and air forces surrounded and captured Baghdad, and the Pentagon declared that major combat in Iraq was over. The second President Bush reached his objective—the overthrow of an ungodly regime, which was threatening the safety of not only its own citizens, but international safety as well. Thankfully, in December of 2003, Saddam Hussein was captured and he will no longer be able to boast about Allah's deliverance; thus, meeting the requirements of our first two premises. The Iraqi people, who were being held captive, were released from the clutches of a killing machine; and the man who represented the demonic power over Iraq was removed (Principles 1 and 2).

The third premise regarding sacrifice was met by the funding of the war, as well as the high prices paid by the men and women who were willing to lay down their lives, knowingly or otherwise, for a righteous objective. Included in the aspect of sacrifice is the fact that we went to war in spite of contrary international opinion. Although the price appeared to be paid in the natural arena, it was in the spiritual realm that Allah suffered major setbacks.

Chapter 16

WHY PICK AND CHOOSE?

I SUPPOSE AMERICANS HAVE the right or at least the curiosity to ask, "Why does America seemingly pick and choose who she will confront militarily speaking?" This question is premised on the idea that many terrorist-led governments and leaders have gone untouched in recent history. There are false gods and ungodly governmental systems in other places around the globe. People by the millions have died at the hands of cruel dictators.

Once known for its plush mountain views and famous gorillas, today Rwanda is only remembered as the place where one of the worst genocides in the twentieth century occurred. National atrocities also plagued Somalia, Bosnia, Uganda, and a host of other countries. In many, if not all of these situations, the United States stayed its distance. So this question does beg a response.

It appears that our leaders in Washington have made decisions based strictly on politically correct and economic premises. In the next chapter I will discuss the fallacy of being politically correct. However, suffice it to say, that this nation, or any nation for that matter, cannot correct all the ills of the world. That's why we need the gospel of Jesus Christ. The Bible says, "Blessed is the nation whose God is the Lord" (Ps. 33:12). When the true God is not allowed to reign in the affairs of both men and nations, the result is most always inhumanities carried out against humanity.

So, why does America seem to pick and choose who its contestants will be? I believe the answer must be threefold:

1. It depends on the assignment given to our president at the time, based upon his foreign policy (not a justification, but a fact).

2. Some interventions are deemed insignificant in the scheme of the global community (sadly enough).

3. American interests must be safeguarded. If a country either threatens us, or takes decisive terrorist action against us, we respond out of self-defense.

The attack on Sept. 11, 2001 and the subsequent loss of over two thousand American lives, and others, could not be overlooked. Afghanistan (Osama bin Laden) and then Iraq (Saddam Hussein) were seen, not only as national threats to world peace, but as international threats, based upon possible nuclear and chemical warheads, thought to be stockpiled within their borders.

Later, media attention would be focused on the Bush administration's inability to prove that Saddam Hussein was indeed stockpiling weapons of mass destruction prior to America's invasion of Iraq. However, either way, it doesn't matter. The ruler representing the demonic powers at bay had to go—regardless!

Let's face it. We are engaged in the same mentality that ultimately brought God's judgment against Judah in the days of Isaiah the prophet. "Woe unto them that call evil good, and good evil; that put darkness for light, and light for darkness…" (Isa. 5:20). What we label as politically correct, God still calls sin. Sooner or later, sin must be judged according to the standards of our righteous God.

Chapter 17

POLITICALLY CORRECT?

B Y GENERAL DEFINITION, pluralism is the acceptance of all religious and secular thought. It is the "all religions lead to God" mentality. It strips the scriptures of their ultimate authority. Verbal and plenary inspiration is maligned. The Bible is reduced to just another good book. Pluralism hails the Moslem's Koran as an alternate message from the same God of the Bible. This philosophical nightmare coupled with humanism declares men to be gods. It is easy to understand how the Antichrist will be able to dupe much of the world into accepting pluralistic thinking during the Tribulation period. The wheels are already set into motion.

In the Book of Isaiah, chapter 6 is commonly referred to as the "woe" chapter. Six woes or statements of judgment are pronounced upon six types of sin: selfish greed (v. 8); drunken conduct (vv.11–12); mockery at God's power to judge their sin (vv.18–19); distortion of God's moral standards (v. 20); arrogance and pride (v. 21); and perversion of justice (vv. 22–23).

Verse 20 says, "Woe unto them that call evil good and good evil…" On the one hand, society often exalts sin by calling depravity manly strength, or calling immorality and perversion true virtue and commendable freedom. Conversely, society opposes righteousness by calling it evil. Perhaps the best example of this unfortunate trend is the labeling of homosexuality and lesbianism as acceptable alternate lifestyles.

Opponents of such conduct, who adhere to biblical standards of sexual morality, are called bigots who perpetuate obsessive prejudice. Pro-abortion advocates are called sensitive persons with a deep commitment to the rights of women, while active pro-life supporters are called extremists or religious fanatics.

Greg Laurie, author of *The Great Compromise*, writes, "It's as if we, as a nation, have developed an allergic reaction to dealing with the old-fashioned notion of personal responsibility. Not only do we no longer wish to take responsibility for our sins, but now we have even created a new politically correct terminology to define them."[1]

In *The Official Politically Correct Dictionary and Handbook*, authors Henry Beard and Christopher Cerf have offered up a number of entries to define common problems in today's society. The authors have, in effect, re-defined sin.[2]

If your problem is laziness, no problem: you will not be called lazy any longer; now you are simply motivationally dispossessed. If your problem is addiction to drugs or alcohol, no problem: you will not be called an addict any longer; now you are simply a substance abuser or chemically inconvenienced.

If your problem is dishonesty, no problem: you will not be called dishonest any longer; you are now ethically disoriented, morally different, or differently honest. If your problem is promiscuity, no problem: you will not be called promiscuous any longer; now you are sexually active.

If your problem is serial killing, no problem: you will not be called a serial killer any longer; now you are socially misaligned or one who has difficult-to-meet needs. If your problem is shoplifting, no problem: you will not be called a shoplifter any longer; now you are one who engages in non-traditional shopping.

If your problem is sexual perversion, no problem: you will not be called a pervert any longer; now you are termed sexually dysfunctional. If your problem is that you lean toward sado-masochism, no problem: you will not be called a sado-masochist any longer; now you are simply differently pleasured.

Using these new definitions, writes Laurie, even the Ten Commandments may one day be re-written to make them more politically correct. Would you care for examples?[3]

> Instead of "Thou shalt not kill," "You should not be socially misaligned."

Instead of "Thou shalt not steal." "Do not be a non-traditional shopper."

Instead of "Thou shalt not commit adultery." "You shall not be "sexually dysfunctional.""

INVOCATION DELIVERED BEFORE THE KANSAS STATE LEGISLATURE

The following prayer delivered by Pastor Joe Wright before the Kansas State Legislature in Topeka, Kansas, made national headlines in 1996. Rev. Wright is the pastor of Central Christian Church in Wichita. The prayer was actually written by the Rev. Bob Russell, of Southeast Christian Church in Louisville, Kentucky. It, too, poignantly illustrates what Isaiah was referring to.[4]

> Heavenly Father, we come before You today to ask Your forgiveness and to seek Your direction and guidance. We know Your Word says, "Woe to those who call evil good," but that is exactly what we have done. We have lost our spiritual equilibrium and inverted our values. We confess that we have ridiculed the absolute truth of Your Word in the name of moral pluralism.
>
> We have worshiped other gods and called it multiculturalism. We have endorsed perversion and called it an alternate lifestyle. We have exploited the poor and called it a lottery. We have neglected the needy and called it self-preservation. We have rewarded laziness and called it welfare.
>
> In the name of choice we have killed our unborn. In the name of right to life we have killed abortionists. We have neglected to discipline our children and called it building esteem. We have abused power and called it political savvy.
>
> We have coveted our neighbor's possessions and called it taxes. We have polluted the air with profanity and pornography and called it freedom of expression. We have ridiculed the time-honored values of our forefathers and called it enlightenment. "Search us, O God, and know our hearts today. Try us, and show us any wicked way in us. Cleanse us from every sin, and set us free" (Ps. 139:23).
>
> Guide and bless these men and women who have been

> sent here by the people of Kansas, and who have been
> ordained by You to govern this great state. Grant them Your
> wisdom to rule, and may their decisions direct us to the
> center of Your will. I ask it in the name of Your Son, the liv-
> ing Savior, Jesus Christ. Amen.

Politically correct? A thousand times no! We cannot settle for peace at any cost. We must not bow our knees to darkness. Someone aptly stated, "What was sin thirty years ago is IN today." May it not be! We will not turn back in the day of battle. Intercessors rise up and pray like never before. Raise up His righteous banner. Lift up a high standard. "When the enemy comes in like a flood, the Spirit of the Lord will lift up a standard against him" (Isa. 59:19).

God promised Moses, "If thou shalt indeed obey his voice, and do all that I speak; then I will be an enemy unto thine enemies, and an adversary unto thine adversaries" (Exod. 23:22). We will not kiss the ring of the Canaanites, or of Pharaoh, or of Baal, or of "Political Correctness," and certainly not of Allah. Darkness may hate the light, but the darkness cannot prevail against the Church of Jesus. The Lord is with us. Stand tall. Stand for righteousness.

Do not back down when the enemy tries to intimidate you. Be like the high school girl who was asked in a mocking tone of voice, "Why are you still a virgin?" The chaste young lady looked her verbal assailant straight in the eyes and said, "I want to know why you're not a virgin!"

My own daughter was similarly mocked in a Christian school setting. She was ridiculed for allowing her parents' religious convictions to steal her uniqueness. Charity replied, "Unique? I can be like you in ten minutes. None of you can be like me the rest of your lives!" That's my girl!

American troops, we thank you for going to Iraq. Thank you for your willing sacrifice. Thank you for not fainting in the day of battle. Secular history may not acknowledge your great contribution in God's plan of redemption, but there is a God in heaven, the one and only true God, Who keeps accurate records. He is the God of history. You played a strategic role in redemptive history, whether you recognize it or ever acknowledge it. America salutes you; the Church of Jesus Christ honors you!

Chapter 18

ONE BILLION SOULS

REMEMBER, PRINCIPALITIES WORK through personalities. That has been the premise of this whole book. There are two forces at work in the world today—good and evil. Goodness and righteousness emanate from God through Jesus Christ by the Holy Spirit. Evil and unrighteousness emanate from Satan. People are either motivated by the Lord or by the devil. The prophet Isaiah compared our righteousness to "filthy rages" (Isa. 64:6).

God does not love Christians over Moslems, Hindus, Buddhists, or the other world religions and many cults. "For God so loved *the world* that He gave His only begotten Son that whosoever believes in Him should not perish, but have everlasting life" (John 3:16, emphasis added). God loves people! The basic premise of this book, and the real issue with God is that we must choose the "master" of our life. Who will be our boss?

The followers of Mohammed have chosen to follow a false god. We do not hate Moslems; we hate the principalities that deceive over one billion people on this planet. This false god, Allah, who is backed by demonic forces, "has blinded the minds of them which believe not, lest the light of the glorious gospel of Christ, who is the image of God, should shine unto them" (2 Cor. 4:4).

His message is one of hate. He offers no assurance of eternal salvation. When he does, it is complicated by external works that offer no hope or security. Mohammed died in 632 a.d. His bleached bones lie in a grave somewhere. He has no power to save. But the grave where Jesus was buried is empty! He is not there, because three days after He was crucified, the Holy Spirit raised Jesus from the dead, and because He lives, we too, shall live. Jesus gives eternal life to those who place their faith in His finished work on the cross. He is eternal life!

Allah is a god of fear and terrorism who commands destruction upon those who refuse to convert to Islam. But our God promises us a wonderful future. He said in Jeremiah 29:11, "For I know the thoughts that I think toward you, saith the Lord, thoughts of peace, and not of evil, to give you an expected end." There are over one billion Muslims on this planet who pray to a false god five times every day. They need to recognize that Jesus is much more than an inferior prophet. He is the Son of the Almighty Living God, whose blood was shed for their redemption. All unreached people groups have been extended God's grace and forgiveness through Jesus Christ. Iraq needs Jesus! America needs Jesus! The whole world needs Jesus! *You need Jesus!* Call on Him today.

The A-B-C's of Salvation [1]

A. Admit you have sinned.

For all have sinned and come short of the glory of God.
—Romans 3:23

B. Believe in Jesus.

For God so loved the world that he gave his only begotten Son that whosoever believeth in him shall not perish, but have everlasting life.
—John 3:16

C. Confess and leave your sin behind.

If we confess our sins, he is faithful and just to forgive us our sins and to cleanse us from all unrighteousness.
—1 John 1:9

Chapter 19

I HAVE GOOD NEWS!

I N THE FINAL analysis, the god of Islam leaves his followers with no hope, only fear about what happens when they die. According to Islam, a man's fate is determined by his actions. A former Muslim described death this way: "When you die, the angel of death comes and removes your soul from your body. He starts at your toenails and works his way up the body until he finally draws the whole soul out of your mouth. The pain is very intense for those who are evil, but Allah makes it easy for the righteous." (See Surah 79:1–2.)

"Then you go to the grave to wait for the Day of Judgment. The grave can be like a little Paradise, or it will be a place of torture. Allah decides."[1]

Dr. Mark A. Gabriel, a native of Egypt, holds a PhD in Islamic history and culture from Al-Azhar University in Cairo. He chose to follow Jesus after reading the Gospel of Matthew for the first time. As he and a friend contemplated what happens at death, he described their conversation as "one more link in the chain of events that would take me out of Islam and lead me to the true God."[2]

Dr. Gabriel quoted the Quran: "And whomsoever Allah wills to guide, he opens his breast to Islam: and whosoever he wills to send astray, he makes his breast closed and constricted, as if he is climbing up to the sky. Thus Allah puts the wrath on those who believe not" (Surah 6:126; 7:178–179; 32:13). Interestingly, the previous quote from the Quran mentions Allah's breast. One of Jehovah's many titles or attributes refers to Him as El Shaddai, which is interpreted, "Breasted One."[3] This attribute speaks to us regarding the love and protection He affords. We are indeed

97

under the shadow of His wing! This title also speaks of His yearning for us to draw close to Him. He brings overwhelming sufficiency to our lives. He wants to remove all doubts and fears in this life and in the life to come! The most pious Muslims cannot make this claim. They live in fear of this uncertainty.

However, the God of the Bible is different. He gives us both hope and the assurance of eternal life through Jesus Christ. The Bible makes clear His intentions. First Timothy 2:3 and 4 says, "For this is good and acceptable in the sight of God our Savior, who desires all men to be saved and to come to the knowledge of the truth." He does not manipulate through fear, but draws through faith. Unlike the god of Islam, the God of biblical Christianity assures us of eternal life through His Son:

> And this is the testimony: that God has given us eternal life, and this life is in His Son. He who has the Son has life; he who does not have the Son of God does not have life. These things I have written to you who believe in the name of the Son of God, that you may know that you have eternal life, and that you may continue to believe in the name of the Son of God.
>
> —1 JOHN 5:11–13

> This God takes away the fear of death and judgment: "Yea, though I walk through the valley of the shadow of death, I will fear no evil.
>
> —PSALM 23:4

We receive eternal life not because we earn it, but because of God's mercy and favor. Titus 3:5 reminds us that it is "not by works of righteousness which we have done, but according to His mercy He saved us..." You too, can experience God's saving grace. You need not fear death, the grave and eternal separation from God. Jesus has made it possible for you to "know" that your sins are forgiven. Do you have this assurance today?

Will you pray this prayer and mean it from your heart?

Dear Jesus, I believe that You are the Son of God. Thank You for dying on the cross that I may have eternal life. I need not fear death and the grave because You died and rose again for me.

You said that if I confess with my mouth that Jesus is Lord, and believe in my heart that God raised You from the dead, that I would be saved. Thank You, Jesus, for forgiving all my sins. I accept, by faith, what You did for me. Thank You for giving me hope and assurance. Thank You for giving me eternal life. You said that because You live, I too shall live.

I realize Lord, that I could never earn Your favor, so I come to You right now, simply believing Your wonderful promise of salvation. In Jesus' name, amen.

Chapter 20

TODAY'S PROPHETIC VOICES

I N THIS FINAL chapter, Prophet Miller and others, who understand what God is doing in this generation, share their prophetic insights.

PROPHET GLENN MILLER

I prophesy that one of the great events on God's calendar is taking place in the world today. Just as the Iron Curtain fell that hindered the gospel, so will the Islamic wall of deception fall before the light of the saving grace of Jesus Christ, and that hundreds of millions of Muslims will turn to Christ in a relatively short period of time.

We have been, and are now in, a period of time where a series of judgments has been released against the false god Allah. When dealing with Pharaoh, it took a series or a system of ten plagues/judgments to bring down and humiliate the gods of Egypt. Today God has set in motion a series of judgments, one after another, that when completed, will have judged, exposed and humiliated the false god Allah, and will open the door for countless Muslim souls to come to Christ.

Church, hear the word of the Lord: Be prepared! The doors of opportunity are opening wide! Therefore, I call My elect to prepare for an evangelistic focus and thrust into the Islamic nations. I will grant both resources and creative wisdom with regard to the means and methods of spreading the gospel past the barriers of resistance. New technological advances have and will continue to occur in communication fields or arenas that will invade past existing walls of resistance and repressive governments and cultures.

In addition, I am now sending in My representatives and spokespeople under the guise of soldiers, social workers, engineers, contractors, educators, doctors, and other professions whose services may be needed. They will go to meet natural needs, but will have a spiritual mandate to spread the gospel and meet spiritual needs. Now *I* am opening ears and touching hearts that only a short time ago were blind and deaf, but now they will hear.

But hear the word of the Lord: The day is quickly coming when My spiritual warriors will go openly and without pretense to declare My Gospel and multitudes will come to hear. Some will go as martyrs and they will be required to pour out their blood to bring redemption to those who have opposed Me. Their blood will not speak of hatred and evil, but of love and compassion.

I will openly show that the Islamic martyrs of hate have shed their blood to a false, evil and uncaring god. I declare the day will come when My word shall be preached in the Islamic nations as openly as it was preached in Christian nations of the world. I will break down the walls of resistance. The gates of hell will not stand and hundreds of millions of Muslims will turn to My Son and be saved.

Therefore, I again say to My Church, prepare yourselves for this new focus. Sharpen your sword! Sharpen your sword of truth and be prepared to do battle against the Islamic lies.

Make yourselves ready. Prepare teams with the knowledge of the Islamic culture and the false doctrines to which it adheres. Prepare yourselves to declare the truth into that darkness. Be prepared to shine the light of that truth into that darkness. For I say to you, it will be said again in this day that the harvest is ready, but the laborers are few. Those who have ears to hear, I will grant you a great harvest of souls and great will be your reward, says the Lord God Almighty.

Related comments

Make sure you understand that I am not prophesying that

Islam will be no more. We will deal with this battle until Jesus returns, but its ability to hinder the Gospel is being broken. This will open the doors for countless millions of Muslims to come to Christ.

1. In the Scriptures, when spiritual plagues and judgments were released, they had their fulfillment on earth through natural means and manifestations. Therefore, these plagues/judgments being released will manifest themselves through natural disasters and catastrophes, as well as natural wars and conflicts. Allah will be shown as fully inadequate to save those who serve him.

2. We must embrace the understanding that the spiritual battle against the demon principality, Allah, will not be an overnight battle. Just as in the time of Moses and Pharaoh, it took a series of ten plagues/judgments to accomplish God's purpose, so today it will take a series of judgments to bring about God's objectives.

Therefore, we must fortify our minds and be prepared for the raging battle to continue with this enemy long after our objectives are accomplished in Iraq. If greater opposition arises from Islam, we must not lose heart. The days of his power are numbered. God has a solution! He will use greater judgment until the peg is forced to fit the hole.

Just as Pharaoh hardened his heart and would not relinquish control, so it will be with this principality. We can expect major opposition that will cause many to lay down their lives to ultimately accomplish God's objective.

Scripture says:

> They conquered him by the blood of the lamb and by the word of their testimony, for they did not love their life even in the face of death. So be glad, heavens, and those who live in them! How terrible it is for the earth and the sea, because the devil has come down to you with great wrath, knowing that his time is short!
>
> —REVELATION 12:11–12, ISV

3. Just as the plagues/judgment in Egypt grew in intensity and severity, until the yoke was fully broken, so shall the attacks against this principality intensify and continue with increasing severity until this yoke too is broken.

4. Evidence of previous judgments are seen with regard to the overthrow of the Taliban extremists, which has resulted in an open door for change and breakthrough to come to Afghanistan. Another judgment that is now underway concerns Osama bin Laden and al-Qaeda, and will continue until the major leadership has been destroyed and the head of the serpent has been effectively cut off.

5. Matthew 24 indicates that the end times will be marked by great conflict. The Scriptures declare that signs in the heavens will point toward the inevitability of wars and rumors of wars. Interestingly enough, God gave a sign in the heavens on August 26 and 27, 2003, during the Iraqi conflict. Mars and earth came within 34,646 miles of each other, the closest they had been in 59,619 years.

    Mars has always represented a type of war. Indeed, it is not a time for peace; it is time for war! Heaven is serving notice that the days of rebellion are coming to an end. God is strategically attacking every barrier that is hindering the knowledge of His Son going to all men.

6. Just as acts of terrorism by Osama bin Laden and al-Qaeda are triggers to draw the United States and other nations into conflict against Afghanistan and against the entrenched pockets of darkness that represent the extremist Islamic beliefs, there will be other trigger situations that will require a natural military, political, government, economical response to release further judgment and break down this power, Allah. We can, therefore, expect more confrontations in the Middle East, Northern Africa, as well as isolated incidents throughout the world.

BISHOP BILL HAMON

Everything that happens in heaven or earth is based on God's will and decrees. God made man a free moral agent with the power of choice. Mankind can obey God's Word and will or rebel against it. Mankind has done and continues to do many things that God does not want him to do.

However, regardless of men's self-will and rebellion against God's Word, will and ways, God still accomplishes His overall will and purpose in the human race. Based on the times and purposes of God, there is a time and season for every purpose on earth. In the fullness of time, God sent forth His Son to be born of woman. God assigned Abraham's descendants to be in Egypt for several centuries. God decreed seventy years of captivity for Israel in Babylon. When Daniel discovered the seventy years had been accomplished, he began to pray and prophesy the prophecy into active fulfillment.

God has established the human race into families, tribes and nations. The Word says God set their boundaries and destinies. From natural observation it would seem that God is not involved or in control of hardly any of the activities on earth.

Nevertheless, the New Testament repeatedly demonstrates that events prophesied by Old Testament prophets did in fact come to pass. In other words, almost everything that happens on earth is because God spoke that it would be thus and so. The prophets of old prophesied about many nations concerning what they would do and become.

Jesus prophesied that wars between nations would intensify the closer we came to the end of this age. Jesus and Paul talked about building Christ's Church until it becomes a powerful victorious army. This army of saints will be given power to execute God's divine decrees concerning nations of the world. " . . . to execute upon them the judgments written, this honor have all His Saints" (Ps. 149:9). Do you not know that the Saints shall judge the world (1 Cor. 6:2)?

The saints of the Most High shall receive the kingdom and possess the kingdom forever, even forever and forever. Then the kingdom and dominion, and the greatness of the kingdom under the whole heaven shall be given to the saints of the Most High. His kingdom is an everlasting kingdom and all dominions shall serve and obey him/them. A judgment was made in favor of the saints of the Most High, and the time came for the saints to possess the kingdom (Dan. 7:18, 22, 27). The angel declared that the delay should be no longer...then the seventh angel sounded and there were loud voices in heaven saying, The kingdoms of this world have become the kingdoms of our Lord and of His Christ (Rev. 10:6; 11:15). From all of these scriptures it is clear that God has decreed that Jesus and His Church saints shall subdue and possess every kingdom until they all come under the Kingship of Jesus Christ, thereby becoming the Kingdoms of our Lord Jesus and His Church.

It has been divinely decreed that every kingdom of wicked man will be brought down. That means the anti-Christ Muslim regime must be dismantled. The Saints will win the war in the heavenlies and mortal soldiers from a nation/nations of God's choosing will fight and win the war using man's weapons of warfare.

The prophets of God are playing a key role in revealing God's time and purpose for peoples and nations of the world.

KIM CLEMENT

These are things that I see. It is important that the people understand that prophecy is needed to show them the plan of God and the direction in which they should go to aid in God's plan coming to pass. This is what God has said to me:

There will be a baptism of our soldiers in the soil as they fight in the Middle East. They will be baptized in the Jordan River. The Iraqi soldiers will be converted because of the American soldiers.

A Middle Eastern man who is blind and has great influence with the kings of the East, shall be raised up from a Muslim stronghold and be filled with God's Spirit. But he will remain behind the cloth and bring Christ to the kings of the East. I saw him with his hand in the hand of the president of the United States in the year 2007. I have seen visions; there are five demonic strongholds that will have to surrender. The year 2007 shall be a marked year. There will be a massive thing that will take place politically between the USA and the Middle East. This president will have the ability to link his hand with a king of the East who is blind. I don't know if he was blind in only one eye or if he was completely blind, but there is an Islamic leader who is going to emerge and link hands with the president of the USA and this will bring massive wealth to America. Not because of the war, but because of the negotiation, because this man who was hidden behind the cloth will come to Christ. This man will remain hidden behind the cloth and shall not make it known to the Islamic people, the depths of his conversion. In his great influence with billions of dollars, there will be a political agreement. There will be a certain amount of peace between American and the Middle East. For a season there will be mass evangelism there.

Because of what President Bush did, by putting the feet of the American soldiers on the soil of those nations, there will also be the feet of angels that will tread upon the Islamic nations. There will be vindication for this president and vindication for this political power because the next president shall have an even greater influence.

Beyond this summer there will be revelations of truth that shall defy what has been said in the Senate and will defy what has been said by the news media. There will be revelations! God will bring it out. He has brought unity between the United States of America and the United Kingdom, and He will bring unity in the United Nations. He will take those who have produced wine and cause their soil to fail. They will not rise up, not against America!

Daniel saw the beast brought to nothing. John, in the Island of Patmos, saw the beast being brought to nothing. You are living in an exciting time and you will see these visions fulfilled.

Religion has tried to stop God's plan, but it never will, because of one stone, it is the stone of revelation. The church, not the political power, is the power of America.

Know the true church, the church that has entered the

kingdom, and the church that has the keys to the kingdom. This is the power that will overcome the Middle Eastern demonic power. It is not the people of the Middle East who need to be overcome as much as it is the spirit of those nations that have risen up. One little stone shall captivate the heart of many and God will get ride of the "Sauls" who are afraid to rise up against them.

Arafat, your days are numbered! There is a new generation that will be raised up and it will bring peace for a season. Arafat! Your days are numbered, there is a new voice coming forth. God will ignite the Middle East and bring His Spirit upon it. Keep it eternal, don't put it into time because if you do that, you take eternal things and make them temporary.

March 11, 2004 was the beginning of an unusual chain of events in the kingdom of God. On that day, a veil of unbelief was torn apart and an unveiling of the hidden treasures and the revelations will be unleashed upon the Lions and spill over into the Middle–Eastern nations. The Lions are the nations that have acknowledged Christ, regardless of the different structures of their religious beliefs; they acknowledged Christ and He called them "Lion." I can redeem them from religion, but these nations will have an unleashing of God's beautiful mysteries and a mass evangelism will begin in each of those countries.

God said, "I am going to wipe out those who will not listen. You will run, because in the months of August, September and October of 2005, I will bring about such great festivities, because of the breakthrough that shall come and governing powers will be on your side, because of the new elections. They'll try again to do what they did to Bush. They will try again to do the same thing, and they'll accuse of corruption, and they'll accuse of mishandling. Oh, no you don't! You leave it! For that shall not resurrect again! I will stop it in an instant! There will be those who will cry out in agony. The government will be on your side because this shall be a thing that I will grant unto you because I love you and because your heart is pure."

The spirit of Babylon has attempted to control the body of Christ for centuries and now we are seeing the fulfillment of God's Word through Jeremiah and John, the Revelator regarding this spiritual force:

"Before your eyes I will repay Babylon and all who live in Babylonia for all the wrong they have done in Zion, declares the Lord. I am against you, O destroying mountain, you who destroys the whole earth, declares the Lord" (Jer. 51:24).

"And after these things I saw another Angel come down from heaven having great power and the earth was lightened with his glory (illuminated); and he cried mightily with a strong voice saying Babylon the great is fallen and has become the habitation of devils and the hold of every foul spirit and the cage of every unclean and hateful bird" (Rev. 18:1–2).

I believe that this speaks of the downfall of the spirit of Babylon. People are always His first priority and therefore it is not God's will that any perish but that all come to the knowledge of the truth. I believe that anyone under the sway and influence of this spirit can be reached and delivered from the controlling, hateful spirit of religious Babylon.

NOTES

Chapter 1
BEHIND THE STORY

1. *Akron Beacon Journal*, Monday, April 19, 2004, p. 1 and A10.

2. *The Cleveland Plain Dealer*, March 12, 2004, A14.

3. *Akron Beacon Journal*, Monday, April 19, 2004, A10.

4. Jim MacKenzie, *The Almanac*, "High school students have definite opinions on possible war with Iraq," January 29, 2003.

Chapter 2
VEILED IN OBSCURITY

1. David B. Crabtree, *There's Hope for Today* (Daily Devotional), April 18, p. 119.

2. Ibid.

Chapter 3
THE ROLE OF THE PROPHET

1. Donald C. Stamps, editor, *The Full Life Study Bible* (Grand Rapids, Michigan: Zondervan Publishing House, 1992).

2. David Cartledge, *The Apostolic Revolution: The Restoration of Apostles and Prophets in the Assemblies of God in Australia* (Chester Hill, NSW: Paraclete Institute, 2000), 233.

3. Dr. Bill Hamon, *The Eternal Church* (Santa Rosa Beach, FL: Christian International Publishers, 1981).

Chapter 4
HISTORY IS *HIS* STORY

1. Finis Jennings Dake, *Dakes Annotated Reference Bible* (Atlanta, GA: Dake Bible Sales, Inc., 1963).

2. Merrill F. Unger, *Unger's Bible Dictionary* (Chicago, IL: Moody Press, 1979), 1055–1058.

3. Ibid., 1058.

Chapter 5
GOD OF WAR

1. Merrill F. Unger, *Unger's Bible Dictionary* (Chicago, IL: Moody Press, 1979), 172.

Chapter 8
THE PLAGUES OF EGYPT

1. Dan Betzer, *Revivaltime Radio Sermons, 1979,* "Frogs, Mosquitoes and Flies," General Council Assemblies of God, 1980, p. 275

2. Warren B. Maben, Seed of Abraham Web site, "The Ten Plagues of Egypt: What Were They?" Used by Permission.

3. Ibid.

Chapter 9
THE DIABOLICAL DUO

1. Merrill F. Unger, *Unger's Bible Dictionary* (Chicago, IL: Moody Press, 1979), 437.

2. Ibid., 497.

3. *The World Book Encyclopedia,* 1994, World Book, Inc., (Earp, Wyatt, p. 15).

Chapter 11
WHO IS ALLAH? (PART 1)

1. *The Encyclopedia Britannica,* s.v. "Muhammad."

2. Charles Swindoll, *Growing Strong in the Seasons of Life* (Portland, OR: Multnomah Press, 1983).

3. *The Encyclopedia Britannica,* s.v. "Muhammad."

4. C. M. Ward, *Revivaltime Radio Sermons,* 1972.

5. *The Encyclopedia Britannica,* s.v. "Muhammad."

6. Ed Decker, "Islam: Another God? Another Gospel?" Feb., 2003. Available from "Saints Alive in Jesus," www.saintsalive.com.

7. Ibid.

8. Ibid.

9. *The Encyclopedia Britannica,* s.v. "Muhammad."

10. Ed Decker, "Islam, Another God? Another Gospel?"

11. Ibid.

12. Ibid.

Chapter 12
WHO IS ALLAH? (PART 2)

1. Lester Sumrall, *Where was God When Pagan Religions Began?* (Nashville, TN: Thomas Nelson, 1980).

2. G.J.O Moshay, *Who Is This Allah?* (Dorchester House Publications, 1995), 10.

3. Ibid., 13.

4. Ibid., 79.

5. Ibid., 79.

6. Ergun Caner and Emir Caner, *Unveiling Islam* (Grand Rapids, MI: Kregel Publications, 2002), 108. Used by permission of the publisher. All rights reserved.

7. Ibid., 243–244

8. Yeshua Communications Network, 1997–98, "Allah: the Moon God."

9. Ergun Caner and Emir Caner, *Unveiling Islam*, 118.

Chapter 13
THE REAL BATTLEGROUND

1. Francis Frangipane, *The Three Battlegrounds* (Arrow Publications, 1977, by the Lockman Foundation). Used by permission.

Chapter 14
THE FALL OF COMMUNISM

1. Merrill F. Unger, *Unger's Bible Dictionary* (Chicago, IL: Moody Press, 1979), 794.

2. Ibid., 795.

3. Ibid.

Chapter 15
THE "THORN" BETWEEN TWO BUSHES

1. Biography of George H. W. Bush, http://www.whitehouse.gov./history/presidents/gb41.html, 2003, A&E Television Network.

2. Ibid.

3. Ibid.

4. Biography of William Jefferson Clinton, http://www.whitehouse.gov/history/presidents/bc42.html, 2003, A&E Television Network.

5. Merrill F. Unger, *Unger's Bible Dictionary* (Chicago, IL: Moody Press, 1979), 416.

6. William Jefferson Clinton, 2003, A&E Television Network.

7. See www.thechurchofchrist.com/roman_empire.htm.

8. "How Many Homosexuals?" An update on homosexual studies based on a 1994 survey. See http://www.lionking.org/~kovu/bible/section 14.html

9. Ibid.

10. Human Rights Campaign, "Wyoming Gay Bashing Victim Matthew Shepard Pronounced Dead," Monday, October 12, 1998. See http://www.hrc.Org/newsreleases/1998/981012mattshepard.asp.

11. Biography of George W. Bush, http://search.biography.com/print record, 2003, A&E Television Network.

12. Ibid.

Chapter 17
POLITICALLY CORRECT?

1. Greg Laurie, *The Great Compromise* (Word Publishing, 1994), 16–17.

2. Ibid., 16.

3. Ibid., 17.

4. Joe Wright, "Invocation Delivered Before the Kansas State Legislature," Topeka, Kansas, 1996.

Chapter 18
ONE BILLION SOULS

1. *Today's Pentecostal Evangel*, "The ABC's of Salvation," January 12, 2003, p. 26

Chapter 19
I HAVE GOOD NEWS!

1. Dr. Mark A. Gabriel, "Muslims and the Afterlife," *Charisma* Magazine, January, 2004, p. 62.

2. Ibid.

3. *El Shaddai: the Breasted One, or Who's That Lady?*, http://www.goodnewsinc.net/v4gn/shaddai.html/.

About the Authors

Prophet Glenn Miller

Since 1973, Glenn Miller's powerful prophetic anointing and bold messages have proven to captivate and greatly edify the body of Christ. His passion reflects the call and heartbeat from the Throne of God for each individual and church body to fulfill their destiny and demonstrate the kingdom of God in every area of their lives.

Foremost in his heart is his mandate to encourage and enable believers to step into a commitment to fulfill their destiny and high call in Christ Jesus, and to leave behind the disappointing and mundane Christian life that has been relegated to them by religion. On numerous occasions the Lord has used the breaker anointing in which Glenn operates to break strongholds off individuals, families, churches and entire regions; thus, releasing and bringing forth promotion and new levels of kingdom living. The Lord releases through him a true apostolic authority to free churches and thrust them into their call and destiny in God.

Glenn travels extensively sharing his messages and changing lives. For over fourteen years he was the pastor of a successful church, until 1990, when God called him to full-time travel. In addition to a bachelor's degree in theology and intensive training under Dr. Bill Hamon of Christian International Ministries, Glenn is ordained as a Christian International Network of Churches (CINC) minister and currently serves on its Board of Governors. He also holds leadership with and presides as a member of the board of governors for many other major ministry groups in the country.

He is co-founder, along with his wife Sherilyn Hamon Miller, and president of Lion's Share Ministries, Inc. He and his wife have four children: Charity, Joshua, Daniel, and Joseph. For the last two years they have lived in and based their ministry out of Pensacola, Florida.

Pastor Roger Loomis

Roger Loomis, an ordained Assemblies of God pastor, has served churches in North Carolina, Alabama, and Ohio since 1978. He is a graduate of Evangel University in Springfield, Missouri. Presently, he and his wife Lori, pastor the Cross Community Church in Elyria, Ohio. They have four children and two grandchildren.

Roger has written for several publications over the years. He completed his autobiography, *The Amazing Power of Touch* in the fall of 2003. In addition, he edits books for Good News to the Nations, a nationally-acclaimed prophetic ministry based out of Atlanta, Georgia.

TO CONTACT THE AUTHORS

Lion's Share Ministries
4600 Mobile Hwy
Suite 9, Box 351
Pensacola, FL 32506
Phone: 850-944-3257
Fax: 850-944-3202
www.lionsshareministries.com
E-mail: lionssharemin@aol.com